THE ESSENTIAL
T.S. ELIOT

THE ESSENTIAL

T.S. ELIOT

Selected and with an Introduction by
VIJAY SESHADRI

An Imprint of HarperCollins*Publishers*

HarperCollins books may be purchased for educational, business, or sales promotional use. For information, please email the Special Markets Department at SPsales@harpercollins.com.

FIRST EDITION

Designed by Renata De Oliveira

Library of Congress Cataloging-in-Publication Data has been applied for.

ISBN 978-0-06-297811-0

20 21 22 23 24   LSC   10 9 8 7 6 5 4 3 2 1

CONTENTS

INTRODUCTION

*I*n 1917, *T.S. Eliot published,* in a print run of five
hundred that didn't sell out until five years later,
his first book of poems, *Prufrock and Other Ob-
servations.* As with a lot of first books by young poets,
the publication of *Prufrock* had a little of a made-in-
the-hood, let's-put-on-a-show quality to it. The book
wasn't actually a book but a pamphlet, and the pub-
lishing house wasn't actually a publishing house but a
London periodical, *The Egoist. The Egoist* is recognized
now as a short-lived and astounding incubator of liter-
ary modernism. Then it was one of the tribal organs of a
small, youthful or recently youthful, "advanced" coterie

of intellectuals and artists who were sure they were doing something new but (except for James Joyce) probably didn't know exactly what it was they were doing and couldn't have imagined how significant they would become. A contributing spirit of the periodical was Eliot's coconspirator and pal Ezra Pound, in his goofy and benevolent village-explainer period rather than his ugly and malevolent world-explainer period or his shattered and tragic self-explainer one. He prevailed on the magazine to lend its imprint to *Prufrock,* and, also, subsidized the publication with money he got from his wife. The literature Pound loved he loved so much it might have seemed to him that he was its author. He'd announced, a little mystifyingly, that Eliot had modernized himself on his own (Pound was a big modernizer) and had appointed himself Eliot's manager. Eliot, with his customary passivity—which was also cagey; Pound nicknamed him Possum—seemed fine with letting Ezra think he was Ezra's invention.

One of the first reviewers of *Prufrock*—again, as is often the case with first books—was a friend of the poet's, Conrad Aiken (who became a major poet himself). The Eliot biographer Peter Ackroyd says that Aiken knew what Eliot was up to better than Pound did. Aiken had known Eliot since college, but sustained friendship doesn't seem to have compromised his appraisals. He says in his review that the author of *Prufrock* is a "bafflingly peculiar man." This bafflingly peculiar person was launching his literary career in a time that was going to make him radically more peculiar—though not more baffling (which word implies a problem still looking for its solution, and a perplexity that might, eventually, be resolved) but, instead, enigmatic (which word implies something active and energetic, and a mystery that we can't pluck the heart out of). The Eliot who could be called baffling was Eliot circa 1914, the writer of the *Prufrock* poems, which were written before the war and peopled by Bostonians. He was like a character in a Henry James story, with a foot in America, a foot in Europe, and a hypertrophied brain living somewhere unmappable. He was, almost comically, a revised, new-century version of James's Gilded Age poor, sensitive gentleman—hardworking, but an intellectual drifter; hiding out in graduate school; trying to keep his parents off his back while depending on their subsidies; prissy and jejune. By 1917, though, he'd stepped from Jamesian fictional paradigms to other, more harrowing ones (though James can be pretty harrowing). He was saying about himself, "I have been living in one of Dostoevsky's novels."

What happened? One answer is that Eliot had relinquished the camouflage of those vanities that he insinuated into the character of Prufrock—the satiric armor disguising a youthful insecurity, the self-satisfied conceit that the world was comatose when it wasn't absurd, the faux French Symbolist weariness. He was now plunged in karma (a word he would have accepted; and an idea that doesn't represent reward or payback but defines the circulating force and interactions of a moral and spiritual ecosystem). He wasn't disembodied anymore, dispersed, arrested, paralyzed, superannuated—"a pair of ragged claws scuttling across the floors of silent seas"— and had outgrown his equivocating, temporizing, he's-finding-himself period (which, to be fair, produced great poetry). He'd made a leap of faith and was dealing with its karmic consequences. He was, in fact, discovering consequentiality itself, and arriving at those first operative adult realizations about the nature of time and change that, twenty years later, would find their place in the beautiful, encircling, Heraclitian meditations of the *Four Quartets*. Eliot's early interest in Indian texts, though benign and as much philological as speculative, was what we would now call Orientalist, and was unreconstructed by our standards. (Later, in his partiality for hymns to imperialism like Kipling's "Recessional"— where the "lesser breeds without the Law" make their appearance—the Orientalism took on a pernicious tinge.) But his study of Vedanta had at least the advantage of giving him a developed understanding of illusion and an appreciation for the complex and subtle laws of action and reaction, change and permanence. (Around this time, he was actually thinking of becoming a Buddhist.)

He'd recently got married—impetuously and, it turned out, disastrously—to Vivienne Haigh-Wood, an English girl who was what used to be called "nervous" (he could have been described that way, too), whom he'd met through an American friend. He had responsibilities. He was a breadwinner, a published poet, and a working reviewer and essayist who supplemented his meager writerly income with a day job in a bank. He was hanging out with Bertrand Russell and Virginia Woolf and other formidable people whose sophistication had a savage quality to it, which it was his obligation to survive. (Russell, under the guise of friendship and solicitude for the young, struggling couple, wound up seducing Vivienne.) His feet and head were finally in the same place, in London, which was in England, which was in Europe, and he was experiencing the tensions and pressures of literary commerce; the anomie of office work in a vast capitalist enterprise (Lloyd's of London); and the anguish of a marriage quickly becoming a source of arduous, painful, confusing dramas and entanglements. (Looking back after Vivienne's death, in 1947, he was to say, "To her the marriage brought no happiness . . . To me it brought the state of mind out of which came *The Waste Land*.")

A more significant answer, though, more significant than his domestic agonies to the question of Eliot's state of mind, more significant than the dolor of office life and the struggle to build a career, was, of course, the war, the First World War, the war to end all wars. As far as great art can be explained, it is the war that explains the riveting, destabilizing drama, bitterly accurate irony, prophetic judgment, ominous atmosphere, and nervously alive and enveloping crepuscularity, at once melancholy, desperate, baleful, unnerving, and vulnerable, of "The Waste Land."

It has mostly gone without saying in the critical tradition that Eliot can't be understood or appreciated without understanding the effect the war had on him. It has mostly gone without saying because the war has been understood as a given and has been said to explain everyone at or around Eliot's age who came into contact with it. But the specificity and emotional intensity of what Eliot achieved in "The Waste Land"— probably the most influential poem of the English language—is imperfectly served if the poem is seen as another artifact of the Lost Generation. The effect of the war on Eliot is an inexhaustible subject. No other work of art in the West of the stature of "The Waste Land" is so immediately and intimately wedded to a major historical cataclysm while being, moreover, radical (in the original meaning of the word) enough, at once close enough and distant enough, imaginative enough, ingenious enough, unreminiscent and unprecedented enough to take the measure of human catastrophe of that order. Pound might have been thinking of

"The Waste Land" when he said that poetry was news that stays news.

Industrialized warfare had been around for a hundred years or more, but the Western world, and the world of Eliot's London generation, was now introduced with a vengeance to its fullest development in its most mechanized and inhuman form. Eliot was a noncombatant. (He tried, and failed, because of a series of bureaucratic impediments, to enlist after America entered the war in April of 1917.) But though he didn't see action, he was in his way as much a war poet as Wilfred Owen or Robert Graves (something that couldn't be said about Pound). The war didn't just, as he might have put it in a laconic moment, modify his sensibilities. The war invaded him and imprinted itself onto his deeper psychic layers. "The Waste Land" is overpowering in its sense of the isolation of the spirit trapped in violent materiality. That sense isn't derived from a Vedantic predilection for seeing life as a painful illusion or a Gnostic antipathy to the body (though these are functional elements in the poem) but is a local and particular response, however circuitous the development, long the gestation, and indirect the realization, to the experience of witnessing, only a few steps removed, systematized carnage.

The reports Eliot was getting in 1917 were gruesome. Here is an example, a battlefield description from a letter written by a soldier in the trenches, which letter was enclosed in a cover letter written on June 17, 1917, and sent to the British magazine *The Nation,* which published it on June 23:

> . . . *a leprous earth, scattered with the swollen and blackening corpses of hundreds of young men. The appalling stench of rotting carrion mingled with the sickening smell of exploded lyddite and ammonal. Mud like porridge, trenches like shallow and sloping cracks in the porridge—porridge that stinks in the sun. Swarms of flies and bluebottles clustering on the pits of offal. Wounded men lying in the shell holes among the decaying corpses: helpless under the scorching sun and bitter nights, under repeated shelling. Men with bowels dropping out, lungs shot away, with blind, smashed faces, or limbs blown into space. Men screaming and gibbering. Wounded men hanging in agony on the barbed wire, until a*

friendly spout of liquid fire shrivels them up like a fly
in a candle. But these are only words, and probably
convey a fraction of their meaning to the hearers.
They shudder, and it is forgotten.

The writer of the cover letter to *The Nation* was
Eliot himself. The letter that he enclosed was writ-
ten by his brother-in-law, Maurice Haigh-Wood, who
had been on the front since before he was nineteen.
(Maurice Haigh-Wood survived the war.) Along with
the terror and agony, the pity and rage that a descrip-
tion like this invokes, Eliot must have had reactions
consistent with the peculiar person he was. A char-
acteristic of his essays is a strong, though mostly
unexamined, metaphoric physicalism in the language
he uses to think about art and culture, along with hints
of an underlying sense that literature produces effects
that are best analyzed if we approach them with analo-
gies drawn from science. In his most famous essay,
"Tradition and the Individual Talent," he compares
the poetic imagination to a filament of platinum that
catalyzes a chemical reaction. This way of thinking
might well have been derived from a psychosomatic

susceptibility. As deeply attuned to moods and impressions as he was, as attuned to verbal acts and as open and vulnerable to the images made by words, as high-strung as he was, Eliot probably responded to language that affected him in ways that seemed physical; and had feelings that would have poisoned him in just the way he says, in his essay on the play, that Hamlet's life and capacity to act were poisoned because of feelings he couldn't articulate or objectify. Eliot must have felt accounts like the passage in the letter previously quoted as illnesses. Strange as it may seem, given how tormented the poem is, how bitter its ironies are, the cure to those illnesses, the release by articulation and objectification, was the shape-shifting, gravitationally dense, translucent, hypnotic, strangely radiating musical orb that is "The Waste Land."

T.*S. Eliot had as much* cultural authority during his lifetime as any writer of any era in the history of the English language. That authority tends to occlude for us the crisis-ridden poet in whom "The Waste Land" was growing. It's hard to discern that Eliot among all the other Eliots who have lived in the literary and public mind for the most of the past hundred years. Eliot the setter of standards. Eliot the lawgiver. Eliot the elitist, lover of rank and hierarchy. Eliot the Defender of the Faith. Eliot the establishmentarian—"classicist in literature, royalist in politics, anglo-catholic in religion." The sporadically, depressingly, dishearteningly anti-Semitic Eliot. The Christian Eliot. The Christian-identity Eliot. Eliot the incomparable literary analyst, who created a whole climate of opinion. Eliot the supercilious literary analyst who made preposterous (but perfectly timed) invidious judgments in passing ("About Donne there hangs the shadow of the impure motive"; "Hazlitt, who had perhaps the most uninteresting mind of all our distinguished critics"). Eliot the editor. Eliot the gatekeeper. Eliot the playwright. Eliot the prizewinner. Eliot the snob. Eliot the intellectual show-off. Eliot, who was turned into a statue by the time he was fifty, and then was put on a plinth and buried up to his neck, like a Beckett character buried in sand, by a storm of critical attention. Eliot the celebrity, friend of Groucho Marx.

But even if we could see that young poet (young as far as poetry is concerned), we still probably would only see the enigma more plainly, and not uncover much of anything useful about him—useful in the sense of satisfying a curiosity about the paths by which intense experience is turned into art, in the way, for example, that Keats's letters are useful. This is because Eliot doesn't share. His own letters—at least the ones that his estate has been recently publishing—are, with rare exceptions, like the one excerpted earlier (in which he is quoting someone else), uninformative, and are consistent with the person who was the orchestrator of his own absence. (Not for nothing did the critic Hugh Kenner call his Eliot book *The Invisible Poet*.) To no other great writer of his era have we as readers a personal relationship, an emotional identification, that is so tenuous. Eliot isn't "relatable." He doesn't invite companionship. He's the most guarded of the modernist writers, the most vigilant about patrolling the no-man's-land between the self and what it creates. We know those other writers, arguably, in the ways we know the people in our lives. The reticent, "classical" ones, like Cavafy, and the ones who inhabit masks or fables, like Pessoa or Kafka (all three of whom have more than a little in common with Eliot when it comes to their rhetorical choices), we know as well as we know the ones who, like Proust or

Lawrence, were prone to be autobiographical. Even saying we don't know him like we know the others seems not true or false but, instead, the product of a conceptual mistake, a category error, and an error that he could have predicted. The famous sentences from "Tradition and the Individual Talent" read: "Poetry is not a turning loose of emotion, but an escape from emotion; it is not the expression of personality, but an escape from personality. But, of course, only those who have personality and emotions know what it means to want to escape from these things."

Like Flaubert's God, Eliot is everywhere present in his work but nowhere apparent. He transformed the rectitude characteristic of the Puritan culture from which he came into a principle by which to govern the artifacts of his imagination, and he applied that principle with impressive consistency. Eliot the person functions as the vanishing point of the long perspective lines of his poetry. Even when he puts himself, rather than a dramatic persona, in his poems, that self is, when it isn't just the grammatical subject, either the existential self of the penitential lyrics or the transcendental subjectivity of the late meditations. The accidental location of that subject in geography and history is the fluorescent dye that allows us to detect the motion of time and reveals the contours of a spiritual topography.

Instead of personality, Eliot draped a transparent veil over his material, one that has optic properties that shrink, elongate, or magnify the enclosed dramatic and symbolic action, and impart a hyperreal clarity (though not a simplicity—Eliot is a "difficult" poet, whose difficulty is fundamental) to that action. Instead of emotion, we are given what he famously called its objective correlative—"a set of objects, a situation, a chain of events which shall be the formula of that *particular* emotion." The force of "The Waste Land" is inseparable from the impersonality of this correlative. Its impersonality is crucial to its aura of perpetual freshness—and the impression it gives that it is permanent—which it has never lost. In fact, in its postapocalyptic, dystopic atmosphere, its gender-bending, its bitter consciousness of sexual violence perpetrated on women, "The Waste Land" is not only news that has stayed news but also current events.

"The Waste Land" also proposes new ideas about

poetry that are as thrilling as ever. The opening passage, introduced by the indelible first line, is like the Louis Armstrong trumpet cadenza that opens the Hot Five's "West End Blues," announcing, with the same ringing articulation, the birth of an art form. The disenchanted vision both opposes and reinforces, and is reinforced by, the energy of the transitions, their unexpectedness, and the joy (a strange but appropriate word to use in the context of a work so dark) their juxtapositions excite. When "The Waste Land" was published, its techniques of collage and multivocality and its cross-cultural, globalized field of reference were as striking as its transitions. Over time, because Eliot taught us a new way of assimilating knowledge into poems, those elements have become familiar. The transitions, though, are as radical as ever and, paradoxically, as inevitable because they both create and are created by the fragmentation of the poem's surface. One of the achievements of "The Waste Land"—and of modernism from Cézanne on—is to make form equal to content as a bearer of significance. The violence inside the poem, the violence experienced by the civilization for which "The Waste Land" is a lamentation, is made vivid to us as much by the abrupt leaps the poem makes from fragment to fragment as by the representation of the effects of that violence on the poem's personas.

Eliot disassembled the poem of his time. He disassembled not just the normative Edwardian-Victorian poem of his time but, also, the "advanced" poem of his time. Texts like "The Comedian as the Letter C" and "Le Cimetière marin," both of which were published almost concurrently and were considered radical in their day, seem, looking back, late Romantic, like the music of Elgar or Richard Strauss, when compared with "The Waste Land." Rather than Stevens or Valéry, the figures of his era with whom Eliot has, at least in the years before his conversion to Anglo-Catholicism, the most in common are probably (as unlikely as it sounds) Duchamp and Brecht. A conceptual, deconstructionist irony governs everything from the actions and transactions of "The Waste Land" to the tongue-in-cheek endnotes—which pull the rug out from under the reader, which "alienate" the reader from the experience he or she or they have just had. The conceptual elements, combined with the impersonality and the philosophical skepticism characteristic of Eliot even in his period of faith and Christian apologetics (he was as well trained in philosophy as any poet in the history of the West), create a separation not only between the poem and the poet and the poem and the reader but, also, between the poem and itself.

The innovations of "The Waste Land," though they were Eliot's, came out of the collective European mind in the aftermath of the war. That they happened doesn't seem mysterious now. What is mysterious is the way the radical new ideas about movement and development, the conceptual superstructures, and the scholarly apparatus engender a deeper unity and integration and enhance and intensify the poem's revelatory power. Many people have imitated Eliot, but no one has been able to reassemble along new lines and reintegrate so completely what was so energetically disassembled. Part of this has to do with Pound's brilliant editing of the poem (which Eliot never failed to acknowledge), but only a part. There is something inherent in the work that makes it whole. That something derives from its mood and music. Eliot was a master of mood, and mood gives the poem a binding energy and reconciles its fragments into an emotional whole. Eliot had a profound sense of musical structure, which everywhere sustains the development and modifies the jaggedness and abruptness of the drama. "The Waste Land" is filled with passages and effects in which the musical satisfaction is as rich and complete as the literary satisfaction. One is the wonderful broken chord at the end of the first stanza that occasions the shifting of grammatical moods from the declarative to the interrogative that begins the second stanza, and that creates a shock of delight. Another astonishing example is the sostenuto ("Ganga was sunken, and the limp leaves / Waited for rain . . .") that initiates the tremendous fable of the thunder that closes the poem. The withdrawal of tension and the narrative soft-pedaling there, before the poem engages its final crescendo, is as exquisite a fusion as there is in poetry of dynamics and rhythm with meaning, myth, and image.

*E*zra Pound was said to have a golden ear. Eliot's ear was better. His diction occupies a sweet spot between the demotic and the aristocratic, and, because of the tension between them, remains convincing, without a trace of the archaic or the futuristic, as close to or as far away from the diction of the twenty-first century as it is from the diction of the twentieth or the nineteenth. The rhythms of the poems, early and late, are local and global. A diffident meter runs evenly just under the surface of the lines and phrases—a beautifully quiet but unwavering metrical presence. An overall sound design disciplines and enlivens each syllable of the poems. The French Symbolists, who were Eliot's first poetic influence, wanted poetry not just to be musical but to arrive at the abstract condition of music. Eliot's poetry arrives at that condition and arrives there without sacrificing for the sake of abstraction, for the sake of a purely musical motive and a meaning that is internal to the text, what he saw as also essential to poems—stories, characters, dramas, human voices, concrete meaning, psychological states, pictures of the world.

Eliot is an American poet. People have said it before: only an American could have come up with his idea of Europe when he came up with it. The other American poet, the other great American poet, who has an ear comparable to his is not Pound but Walt Whitman. Whitman's sonic education was ahistorical and biblical, while Eliot's derived directly from the study of English prosody and its classical antecedents. Whitman was writing operas and symphonies with large forces. Eliot was writing chamber music, implicitly in the beginning and explicitly at the end, in the "Four Quartets." But like Eliot, Whitman had a mastery of wide sonic intervals; a terrific ability to modulate between large- and small-scale aural effects; and a wonderful purity, a delicacy, and a delicate control, of tone, a natural diction that never grows stale. And in both Eliot and Whitman the individual notes and the chords resonate in a vast echo chamber where sound itself has a spiritual meaning.

This introduction to Eliot's poems is being written in the bicentennial year of Whitman's birth. It's tempting in this context to triangulate Eliot the poet by means of Whitman. It's also apt and useful. It's also addictive. Once the comparison is made it can't be shaken off. It says a lot about the poets, about poetry, and about America. The contrasts are so sharp that by them alone the comparison is justified. Whitman's rhetoric is frank and personal. Eliot's is the opposite. Whitman repeats himself. Eliot never does. To say that Eliot had even a passing enthusiasm for democracy would be to stretch credulity. Whitman was self-educated. Eliot had the best institutional education available in the America of his time. Whitman is the poet of happiness as decisively as Eliot is the poet of unhappiness. They exist at the opposite poles of spiritual life. God hangs out with Whitman. God is Whitman's homey. Whitman presupposes God. Even in his most intense spiritual writing, Eliot infrequently and gingerly mentions God. The mystical union in Whitman is like a function of his body, as inevitable as breathing. Eliot's poetry, on the other hand, from "The Waste Land" on, is the enactment of a journey along the *via negativa,* the path of penitence, abnegation, suffering, dark nights of the soul, the path that traverses the stony places, passes by empty cisterns and exhausted wells, through dead lands, cactus lands, valleys of dying stars. "The Waste Land" poses a question to which only God could be the answer. All the major poems Eliot writes after "The Waste Land" are singular events—defined by rhetorical and metrical inventions designed for those events alone—that document the stages of a search for that answer, one that is excruciating, carried on in both hope and doubt. And as rich and round as it is, as satisfying to the mind, the beatific vision, when Eliot finally arrives at it in the *Four Quartets*, is muted, solemn, intellectual, and diffident even in its ecstasy.

We love Whitman, and we don't love Eliot—or, rather, we don't seem to be able to establish that personal relationship to Eliot that would be a necessary condition of our loving him. Whitman insists on that personal relationship. Eliot forbids it. But love isn't why we read poetry. Poetry is why we read poetry. To separate ourselves from the enchantments or disenchantments these two central makers of American poetry impose on us, and to see them just as their poetry makes it possible to recognize how much they actually have in common, Whitman's imposition of friendship on his readers is as much a rhetorical trick as Eliot's forbidding that same friendship. Both poets disappear into their poems, as all great poets do, whatever the fiction they use to address the reader. Eliot is thought of as a cold poet, but it can be convincingly argued that Whitman is, too. (We disdain Eliot's politics, and think of Whitman as our representative—though Whitman was tickled pink to see America steal large chunks of Mexico and contemplated with impassive neutrality the extinction of American Indians by the onslaught of Manifest Destiny.)

And, beyond this, the similarities cascade: Both were revolutionary, and both were original—which aren't the same thing. The techniques and possibilities of poetry were vastly expanded by both of them. They were both visionary, and they were both public figures, teachers of their visions. Both were transformed by living through a bloody and terrible war. The scale of their ambition was enormous and exactly the same, and they both, astonishingly, realized that ambition. They were both committed to a transcendental motive, one derived from their common nonconformist American religious culture. They both believed life is a spiritual experience, and poems are meant to embody that experience. They can be seen as companions. To say it again, we read poetry for poetry, and on that basis if it's an honor for Eliot to be thought of as a good companion for Whitman it's just as much an honor for Whitman. They belong together in important ways, in essential ways. In their influence on others and on the culture at large, there are no other American poets quite like them. One of the singular insights Eliot has in "Tradition and the Individual Talent" is the phenomenological paradox that the present changes the past. Our present, our woke present, democratic, aware of positionalities, alive to difference, requiring at least the rhetorical gestures of frankness, openness, tends to cling to Whitman and not to Eliot. Our present, though, has many elements that Eliot understood but Whitman didn't. In fact, in his urban angst, his apocalyptic consciousness, his feeling for the real dangers of experience, his recognition that spiritual insight is not a joy, or not a joy only, but a terrible necessity, it just might be Eliot who has stopped somewhere and is waiting for us.

—*Vijay Seshadri*

THE ESSENTIAL
T.S. ELIOT

LA FIGLIA CHE PIANGE

O quam te memorem virgo . . .

Stand on the highest pavement of the stair—
Lean on a garden urn—
Weave, weave the sunlight in your hair—
Clasp your flowers to you with a pained surprise—
Fling them to the ground and turn
With a fugitive resentment in your eyes:
But weave, weave the sunlight in your hair.

So I would have had him leave,
So I would have had her stand and grieve,
So he would have left
As the soul leaves the body torn and bruised,
As the mind deserts the body it has used.
I should find
Some way incomparably light and deft,
Some way we both should understand,
Simple and faithless as a smile and shake of the hand.

She turned away, but with the autumn weather
Compelled my imagination many days,
Many days and many hours:
Her hair over her arms and her arms full of flowers.
And I wonder how they should have been together!
I should have lost a gesture and a pose.
Sometimes these cogitations still amaze
The troubled midnight and the noon's repose.

PORTRAIT OF A LADY

Thou hast committed—
Fornication: but that was in another country,
And besides, the wench is dead.

THE JEW OF MALTA.

I

Among the smoke and fog of a December afternoon
You have the scene arrange itself—as it will seem to do—
With 'I have saved this afternoon for you';
And four wax candles in the darkened room,
Four rings of light upon the ceiling overhead,
An atmosphere of Juliet's tomb
Prepared for all the things to be said, or left unsaid.
We have been, let us say, to hear the latest Pole
Transmit the Preludes, through his hair and finger-tips.
'So intimate, this Chopin, that I think his soul
Should be resurrected only among friends
Some two or three, who will not touch the bloom
That is rubbed and questioned in the concert room.'
—And so the conversation slips

Among velleities and carefully caught regrets
Through attenuated tones of violins
Mingled with remote cornets
And begins.
'You do not know how much they mean to me, my friends,
And how, how rare and strange it is, to find
In a life composed so much, so much of odds and ends,
(For indeed I do not love it . . . you knew? you are not blind!
How keen you are!)
To find a friend who has these qualities,
Who has, and gives
Those qualities upon which friendship lives.
How much it means that I say this to you—
Without these friendships—life, what *cauchemar!*'

Among the windings of the violins
And the ariettes
Of cracked cornets
Inside my brain a dull tom-tom begins
Absurdly hammering a prelude of its own,
Capricious monotone
That is at least one definite 'false note.'

—Let us take the air, in a tobacco trance,
Admire the monuments,
Discuss the late events,
Correct our watches by the public clocks.
Then sit for half an hour and drink our bocks.

II

Now that lilacs are in bloom
She has a bowl of lilacs in her room
And twists one in her fingers while she talks.
'Ah, my friend, you do not know, you do not know
What life is, you who hold it in your hands';
(Slowly twisting the lilac stalks)
'You let it flow from you, you let it flow,
And youth is cruel, and has no remorse
And smiles at situations which it cannot see.'
I smile, of course,
And go on drinking tea.

'Yet with these April sunsets, that somehow recall
My buried life, and Paris in the Spring,
I feel immeasurably at peace, and find the world
To be wonderful and youthful, after all.'

The voice returns like the insistent out-of-tune
Of a broken violin on an August afternoon:
'I am always sure that you understand
My feelings, always sure that you feel,
Sure that across the gulf you reach your hand.

You are invulnerable, you have no Achilles' heel.
You will go on, and when you have prevailed
You can say: at this point many a one has failed.
But what have I, but what have I, my friend,
To give you, what can you receive from me?
Only the friendship and the sympathy
Of one about to reach her journey's end.

I shall sit here, serving tea to friends. . . .'

I take my hat: how can I make a cowardly amends
For what she has said to me?
You will see me any morning in the park
Reading the comics and the sporting page.
Particularly I remark
An English countess goes upon the stage.
A Greek was murdered at a Polish dance,
Another bank defaulter has confessed.
I keep my countenance,
I remain self-possessed
Except when a street-piano, mechanical and tired
Reiterates some worn-out common song
With the smell of hyacinths across the garden
Recalling things that other people have desired.
Are these ideas right or wrong?

III

The October night comes down; returning as before
Except for a slight sensation of being ill at ease
I mount the stairs and turn the handle of the door
And feel as if I had mounted on my hands and knees.
'And so you are going abroad; and when do you return?
But that's a useless question.
You hardly know when you are coming back,
You will find so much to learn.'
My smile falls heavily among the bric-à-brac.

'Perhaps you can write to me.'
My self-possession flares up for a second;
This is as I had reckoned.
'I have been wondering frequently of late
(But our beginnings never know our ends!)
Why we have not developed into friends.'
I feel like one who smiles, and turning shall remark
Suddenly, his expression in a glass.
My self-possession gutters; we are really in the dark.

'For everybody said so, all our friends,
They all were sure our feelings would relate

So closely! I myself can hardly understand.
We must leave it now to fate.
You will write, at any rate.
Perhaps it is not too late.
I shall sit here, serving tea to friends.'

And I must borrow every changing shape
To find expression . . . dance, dance
Like a dancing bear,
Cry like a parrot, chatter like an ape.
Let us take the air, in a tobacco trance—

Well and what if she should die some afternoon,
Afternoon grey and smoky, evening yellow and rose;
Should die and leave me sitting pen in hand
With the smoke coming down above the housetops;
Doubtful, for a while
Not knowing what to feel or if I understand
Or whether wise or foolish, tardy or too soon . . .
Would she not have the advantage, after all?
This music is successful with a 'dying fall'
Now that we talk of dying—
And should I have the right to smile?

PRELUDES

I

The winter evening settles down
With smell of steaks in passageways.
Six o'clock.
The burnt-out ends of smoky days.
And now a gusty shower wraps
The grimy scraps
Of withered leaves about your feet
And newspapers from vacant lots;
The showers beat
On broken blinds and chimney-pots,
And at the corner of the street
A lonely cab-horse steams and stamps.

And then the lighting of the lamps.

II

The morning comes to consciousness
Of faint stale smells of beer
From the sawdust-trampled street
With all its muddy feet that press
To early coffee-stands.

With the other masquerades
That time resumes,
One thinks of all the hands
That are raising dingy shades
In a thousand furnished rooms.

III

You tossed a blanket from the bed,
You lay upon your back, and waited;
You dozed, and watched the night revealing
The thousand sordid images
Of which your soul was constituted;
They flickered against the ceiling.
And when all the world came back
And the light crept up between the shutters
And you heard the sparrows in the gutters,
You had such a vision of the street
As the street hardly understands;
Sitting along the bed's edge, where
You curled the papers from your hair,
Or clasped the yellow soles of feet
In the palms of both soiled hands.

IV

His soul stretched tight across the skies
That fade behind a city block,
Or trampled by insistent feet
At four and five and six o'clock;
And short square fingers stuffing pipes,
And evening newspapers, and eyes
Assured of certain certainties,
The conscience of a blackened street
Impatient to assume the world.

I am moved by fancies that are curled
Around these images, and cling:
The notion of some infinitely gentle
Infinitely suffering thing.

Wipe your hand across your mouth, and laugh;
The worlds revolve like ancient women
Gathering fuel in vacant lots.

RHAPSODY ON A WINDY NIGHT

Twelve o'clock.
Along the reaches of the street
Held in a lunar synthesis,
Whispering lunar incantations
Dissolve the floors of memory
And all its clear relations,
Its divisions and precisions.
Every street-lamp that I pass
Beats like a fatalistic drum,
And through the spaces of the dark
Midnight shakes the memory
As a madman shakes a dead geranium.

Half-past one,
The street-lamp sputtered,
The street-lamp muttered,
The street-lamp said, 'Regard that woman
Who hesitates toward you in the light of the door
Which opens on her like a grin.
You see the border of her dress

Is torn and stained with sand,
And you see the corner of her eye
Twists like a crooked pin.'

The memory throws up high and dry
A crowd of twisted things;
A twisted branch upon the beach
Eaten smooth, and polished
As if the world gave up
The secret of its skeleton,
Stiff and white.
A broken spring in a factory yard,
Rust that clings to the form that the strength has left
Hard and curled and ready to snap.

Half-past two,
The street-lamp said,
'Remark the cat which flattens itself in the gutter,
Slips out its tongue
And devours a morsel of rancid butter.'
So the hand of the child, automatic,
Slipped out and pocketed a toy that was running along the quay.
I could see nothing behind that child's eye.
I have seen eyes in the street

Trying to peer through lighted shutters,
And a crab one afternoon in a pool,
An old crab with barnacles on his back,
Gripped the end of a stick which I held him.

Half-past three,
The lamp sputtered,
The lamp muttered in the dark.
The lamp hummed:
'Regard the moon,
La lune ne garde aucune rancune,
She winks a feeble eye,
She smiles into corners.
She smooths the hair of the grass.
The moon has lost her memory.
A washed-out smallpox cracks her face,
Her hand twists a paper rose,
That smells of dust and eau de Cologne,
She is alone
With all the old nocturnal smells
That cross and cross across her brain.'
The reminiscence comes
Of sunless dry geraniums
And dust in crevices,

Smells of chestnuts in the streets,
And female smells in shuttered rooms,
And cigarettes in corridors
And cocktail smells in bars.

The lamp said,
'Four o'clock,
Here is the number on the door.
Memory!
You have the key,
The little lamp spreads a ring on the stair.
Mount.
The bed is open; the tooth-brush hangs on the wall,
Put your shoes at the door, sleep, prepare for life.'

The last twist of the knife.

MR. APOLLINAX

Ὦ τῆς καινότητος.   Ἡράκλεις, τῆς παραδοξολοίας.
εὐμήχανος ἀνθρωπος.

LUCIAN

When Mr. Apollinax visited the United States
His laughter tinkled among the teacups.
I thought of Fragilion, that shy figure among the birch-trees,
And of Priapus in the shrubbery
Gaping at the lady in the swing.
In the palace of Mrs. Phlaccus, at Professor Channing-Cheetah's
He laughed like an irresponsible fœtus.
His laughter was submarine and profound
Like the old man of the sea's
Hidden under coral islands
Where worried bodies of drowned men drift down in the green
    silence,
Dropping from fingers of surf.

I looked for the head of Mr. Apollinax rolling under a chair
Or grinning over a screen
With seaweed in its hair.
I heard the beat of centaur's hoofs over the hard turf
As his dry and passionate talk devoured the afternoon.
'He is a charming man'—'But after all what did he mean?'—
'His pointed ears. . . . He must be unbalanced.'—
'There was something he said that I might have challenged.'
Of dowager Mrs. Phlaccus, and Professor and Mrs. Cheetah
I remember a slice of lemon, and a bitten macaroon.

THE LOVE SONG OF
J. ALFRED PRUFROCK

S'io credesse che mia risposta fosse
a persona che mai tornasse al mondo,
questa fiamma staria senza più scosse.
Ma per ciò che giammai di questo fondo
non tornò vivo alcun, s'i'odo il vero,
senza tema d'infamia ti rispondo.

Let us go then, you and I,
When the evening is spread out against the sky
Like a patient etherised upon a table;
Let us go, through certain half-deserted streets,
The muttering retreats
Of restless nights in one-night cheap hotels
And sawdust restaurants with oyster-shells:
Streets that follow like a tedious argument
Of insidious intent
To lead you to an overwhelming question . . .
Oh, do not ask, 'What is it?'
Let us go and make our visit.

In the room the women come and go
Talking of Michelangelo.

The yellow fog that rubs its back upon the window-panes,
The yellow smoke that rubs its muzzle on the window-panes,
Licked its tongue into the corners of the evening,
Lingered upon the pools that stand in drains,
Let fall upon its back the soot that falls from chimneys,
Slipped by the terrace, made a sudden leap,
And seeing that it was a soft October night,
Curled once about the house, and fell asleep.

And indeed there will be time
For the yellow smoke that slides along the street
Rubbing its back upon the window-panes;
There will be time, there will be time
To prepare a face to meet the faces that you meet;
There will be time to murder and create,
And time for all the works and days of hands
That lift and drop a question on your plate;
Time for you and time for me,
And time yet for a hundred indecisions,
And for a hundred visions and revisions,
Before the taking of a toast and tea.

In the room the women come and go
Talking of Michelangelo.

And indeed there will be time
To wonder, 'Do I dare?' and, 'Do I dare?'
Time to turn back and descend the stair,
With a bald spot in the middle of my hair—
(They will say: 'How his hair is growing thin!')
My morning coat, my collar mounting firmly to the chin,
My necktie rich and modest, but asserted by a simple pin—
(They will say: 'But how his arms and legs are thin!')
Do I dare
Disturb the universe?
In a minute there is time
For decisions and revisions which a minute will reverse.

For I have known them all already, known them all—
Have known the evenings, mornings, afternoons,
I have measured out my life with coffee spoons;
I know the voices dying with a dying fall
Beneath the music from a farther room.
        So how should I presume?

And I have known the eyes already, known them all—
The eyes that fix you in a formulated phrase,
And when I am formulated, sprawling on a pin,
When I am pinned and wriggling on the wall,
Then how should I begin
To spit out all the butt-ends of my days and ways?
     And how should I presume?

And I have known the arms already, known them all—
Arms that are braceleted and white and bare
(But in the lamplight, downed with light brown hair!)
Is it perfume from a dress
That makes me so digress?
Arms that lie along a table, or wrap about a shawl.
     And should I then presume?
     And how should I begin?

    . . .

Shall I say, I have gone at dusk through narrow streets
And watched the smoke that rises from the pipes
Of lonely men in shirt-sleeves, leaning out of windows? . . .

    . . .

I should have been a pair of ragged claws
Scuttling across the floors of silent seas.

        . . .

And the afternoon, the evening, sleeps so peacefully!
Smoothed by long fingers,
Asleep . . . tired . . . or it malingers,
Stretched on the floor, here beside you and me.
Should I, after tea and cakes and ices,
Have the strength to force the moment to its crisis?
But though I have wept and fasted, wept and prayed,
Though I have seen my head (grown slightly bald) brought in
    upon a platter,
I am no prophet—and here's no great matter;
I have seen the moment of my greatness flicker,
And I have seen the eternal Footman hold my coat, and snicker,
And in short, I was afraid.

And would it have been worth it, after all,
After the cups, the marmalade, the tea,
Among the porcelain, among some talk of you and me,
Would it have been worth while,
To have bitten off the matter with a smile,
To have squeezed the universe into a ball

To roll it towards some overwhelming question,
To say: 'I am Lazarus, come from the dead,
Come back to tell you all, I shall tell you all'—
If one, settling a pillow by her head,
    Should say: 'That is not what I meant at all.
    That is not it, at all.'

And would it have been worth it, after all,
Would it have been worth while,
After the sunsets and the dooryards and the sprinkled streets,
After the novels, after the teacups, after the skirts that trail along
    the floor—
And this, and so much more?—
It is impossible to say just what I mean!
But as if a magic lantern threw the nerves in patterns on a
    screen:
Would it have been worth while
If one, settling a pillow or throwing off a shawl,
And turning toward the window, should say:
    'That is not it at all,
    That is not what I meant, at all.'

No! I am not Prince Hamlet, nor was meant to be;
Am an attendant lord, one that will do

To swell a progress, start a scene or two,
Advise the prince; no doubt, an easy tool,
Deferential, glad to be of use,
Politic, cautious, and meticulous;
Full of high sentence, but a bit obtuse;
At times, indeed, almost ridiculous—
Almost, at times, the Fool.

I grow old . . . I grow old . . .
I shall wear the bottoms of my trousers rolled.

Shall I part my hair behind? Do I dare to eat a peach?
I shall wear white flannel trousers, and walk upon the beach.
I have heard the mermaids singing, each to each.

I do not think that they will sing to me.

I have seen them riding seaward on the waves
Combing the white hair of the waves blown back
When the wind blows the water white and black.

We have lingered in the chambers of the sea
By sea-girls wreathed with seaweed red and brown
Till human voices wake us, and we drown.

GERONTION

Thou hast nor youth nor age
But as it were an after dinner sleep
Dreaming of both.

Here I am, an old man in a dry month,
Being read to by a boy, waiting for rain.
I was neither at the hot gates
Nor fought in the warm rain
Nor knee deep in the salt marsh, heaving a cutlass,
Bitten by flies, fought.
My house is a decayed house,
And the Jew squats on the window sill, the owner,
Spawned in some estaminet of Antwerp,
Blistered in Brussels, patched and peeled in London.
The goat coughs at night in the field overhead;
Rocks, moss, stonecrop, iron, merds.
The woman keeps the kitchen, makes tea,
Sneezes at evening, poking the peevish gutter.
                              I an old man,
A dull head among windy spaces.

Signs are taken for wonders. 'We would see a sign!'
The word within a word, unable to speak a word,
Swaddled with darkness. In the juvescence of the year
Came Christ the tiger

In depraved May, dogwood and chestnut, flowering judas,
To be eaten, to be divided, to be drunk
Among whispers; by Mr. Silvero
With caressing hands, at Limoges
Who walked all night in the next room;

By Hakagawa, bowing among the Titians;
By Madame de Tornquist, in the dark room
Shifting the candles; Fräulein von Kulp
Who turned in the hall, one hand on the door.
        Vacant shuttles
Weave the wind. I have no ghosts,
An old man in a draughty house
Under a windy knob.

After such knowledge, what forgiveness? Think now
History has many cunning passages, contrived corridors
And issues, deceives with whispering ambitions,
Guides us by vanities. Think now

She gives when our attention is distracted
And what she gives, gives with such supple confusions
That the giving famishes the craving. Gives too late
What's not believed in, or is still believed,
In memory only, reconsidered passion. Gives too soon
Into weak hands, what's thought can be dispensed with
Till the refusal propagates a fear. Think
Neither fear nor courage saves us. Unnatural vices
Are fathered by our heroism. Virtues
Are forced upon us by our impudent crimes.
These tears are shaken from the wrath-bearing tree.

The tiger springs in the new year. Us he devours. Think at
    last
We have not reached conclusion, when I
Stiffen in a rented house. Think at last
I have not made this show purposelessly
And it is not by any concitation
Of the backward devils.

I would meet you upon this honestly.
I that was near your heart was removed therefrom
To lose beauty in terror, terror in inquisition.
I have lost my passion: why should I need to keep it

Since what is kept must be adulterated?
I have lost my sight, smell, hearing, taste and touch:
How should I use them for your closer contact?

These with a thousand small deliberations
Protract the profit of their chilled delirium,
Excite the membrane, when the sense has cooled,
With pungent sauces, multiply variety
In a wilderness of mirrors. What will the spider do,
Suspend its operations, will the weevil
Delay? De Bailhache, Fresca, Mrs. Cammel, whirled
Beyond the circuit of the shuddering Bear
In fractured atoms. Gull against the wind, in the windy straits
Of Belle Isle, or running on the Horn.
White feathers in the snow, the Gulf claims,
And an old man driven by the Trades
To a sleepy corner.

    Tenants of the house,
Thoughts of a dry brain in a dry season.

DANS LE RESTAURANT

Le garçon délabré qui n'a rien à faire
Que de se gratter les doigts et se pencher sur mon épaule:
    'Dans mon pays il fera temps pluvieux,
    Du vent, du grand soleil, et de la pluie;
    C'est ce qu'on appelle le jour de lessive des gueux.'
(Bavard, baveux, à la croupe arrondie,
Je te prie, au moins, ne bave pas dans la soupe.)
    'Les saules trempés, et des bourgeons sur les ronces—
    C'est là, dans une averse, qu'on s'abrite.
J'avais sept ans, elle était plus petite.
    Elle était toute mouillée, je lui ai donné des primevères.'
Les taches de son gilet montent au chiffre de trente-huit.
    'Je la chatouillais, pour la faire rire.
    J'éprouvais un instant de puissance et de délire.'

Mais alors, vieux lubrique, à cet âge . . .
'Monsieur, le fait est dur.
   Il est venu, nous peloter, un gros chien;
   Moi j'avais peur, je l'ai quittée à mi-chemin.
   C'est dommage.'
      Mais alors, tu as ton vautour!
Va t'en te décrotter les rides du visage;
Tiens, ma fourchette, décrasse-toi le crâne.
De quel droit payes-tu des expériences comme moi?
Tiens, voilà dix sous, pour la salle-de-bains.

Phlébas, le Phénicien, pendant quinze jours noyé,
Oubliait les cris des mouettes et la houle de Cornouaille,
Et les profits et les pertes, et la cargaison d'étain:
Un courant de sous-mer l'emporta très loin,
Le repassant aux étapes de sa vie antérieure.
Figurez-vous donc, c'était un sort pénible;
Cependant, ce fut jadis un bel homme, de haute taille.

WHISPERS OF IMMORTALITY

Webster was much possessed by death
And saw the skull beneath the skin;
And breastless creatures under ground
Leaned backward with a lipless grin.

Daffodil bulbs instead of balls
Stared from the sockets of the eyes!
He knew that thought clings round dead limbs
Tightening its lusts and luxuries.

Donne, I suppose, was such another
Who found no substitute for sense,
To seize and clutch and penetrate;
Expert beyond experience,

He knew the anguish of the marrow
The ague of the skeleton;
No contact possible to flesh
Allayed the fever of the bone.

Grishkin is nice: her Russian eye
Is underlined for emphasis;
Uncorseted, her friendly bust
Gives promise of pneumatic bliss.

The couched Brazilian jaguar
Compels the scampering marmoset
With subtle effluence of cat;
Grishkin has a maisonnette;

The sleek Brazilian jaguar
Does not in its aboreal gloom
Distil so rank a feline smell
As Grishkin in a drawing-room.

And even the Abstract Entities
Circumambulate her charm;
But our lot crawls between dry ribs
To keep our metaphysics warm.

THE WASTE LAND

"Nam Sibyllam quidem Cumis ego ipse oculis meis vidi in ampulla pendere, et cum illi pueri dicerent: Σίβυλλα τί θέλεις; respondebat illa: ἀποθανεῖν θέλω."

I. The Burial of the Dead

April is the cruellest month, breeding
Lilacs out of the dead land, mixing
Memory and desire, stirring
Dull roots with spring rain.
Winter kept us warm, covering
Earth in forgetful snow, feeding
A little life with dried tubers.
Summer surprised us, coming over the Starnbergersee
With a shower of rain; we stopped in the colonnade,
And went on in sunlight, into the Hofgarten,
And drank coffee, and talked for an hour.
Bin gar keine Russin, stamm' aus Litauen, echt deutsch.
And when we were children, staying at the arch-duke's,
My cousin's, he took me out on a sled,
And I was frightened. He said, Marie,
Marie, hold on tight. And down we went.
In the mountains, there you feel free.
I read, much of the night, and go south in the winter.

What are the roots that clutch, what branches grow
Out of this stony rubbish? Son of man,
You cannot say, or guess, for you know only
A heap of broken images, where the sun beats,
And the dead tree gives no shelter, the cricket no relief,
And the dry stone no sound of water. Only
There is shadow under this red rock,
(Come in under the shadow of this red rock),
And I will show you something different from either
Your shadow at morning striding behind you
Or your shadow at evening rising to meet you;
I will show you fear in a handful of dust.

 Frisch weht der Wind
 Der Heimat zu
 Mein Irisch Kind,
 Wo weilest du?

'You gave me hyacinths first a year ago;
'They called me the hyacinth girl.'
—Yet when we came back, late, from the hyacinth garden,
Your arms full, and your hair wet, I could not
Speak, and my eyes failed, I was neither
Living nor dead, and I knew nothing,
Looking into the heart of light, the silence.
Oed' und leer das Meer.

Madame Sosostris, famous clairvoyante,
Had a bad cold, nevertheless
Is known to be the wisest woman in Europe,
With a wicked pack of cards. Here, said she,
Is your card, the drowned Phoenician Sailor,
(Those are pearls that were his eyes. Look!)
Here is Belladonna, the Lady of the Rocks,
The lady of situations.
Here is the man with three staves, and here the Wheel,
And here is the one-eyed merchant, and this card,
Which is blank, is something he carries on his back,
Which I am forbidden to see. I do not find
The Hanged Man. Fear death by water.
I see crowds of people, walking round in a ring.
Thank you. If you see dear Mrs. Equitone,
Tell her I bring the horoscope myself:
One must be so careful these days.
Unreal City,
Under the brown fog of a winter dawn,
A crowd flowed over London Bridge, so many,
I had not thought death had undone so many.
Sighs, short and infrequent, were exhaled,
And each man fixed his eyes before his feet.
Flowed up the hill and down King William Street,

To where Saint Mary Woolnoth kept the hours
With a dead sound on the final stroke of nine.
There I saw one I knew, and stopped him, crying: 'Stetson!
'You who were with me in the ships at Mylae!
'That corpse you planted last year in your garden,
'Has it begun to sprout? Will it bloom this year?
'Or has the sudden frost disturbed its bed?
'O keep the Dog far hence, that's friend to men,
'Or with his nails he'll dig it up again!
'You! hypocrite lecteur!—mon semblable,—mon frère!'

II. A Game of Chess

The Chair she sat in, like a burnished throne,
Glowed on the marble, where the glass
Held up by standards wrought with fruited vines
From which a golden Cupidon peeped out
(Another hid his eyes behind his wing)
Doubled the flames of sevenbranched candelabra
Reflecting light upon the table as
The glitter of her jewels rose to meet it,
From satin cases poured in rich profusion.
In vials of ivory and coloured glass
Unstoppered, lurked her strange synthetic perfumes,
Unguent, powdered, or liquid—troubled, confused
And drowned the sense in odours; stirred by the air
That freshened from the window, these ascended
In fattening the prolonged candle-flames,
Flung their smoke into the laquearia,
Stirring the pattern on the coffered ceiling.
Huge sea-wood fed with copper
Burned green and orange, framed by the coloured stone,
In which sad light a carved dolphin swam.
Above the antique mantel was displayed
As though a window gave upon the sylvan scene

The change of Philomel, by the barbarous king
So rudely forced; yet there the nightingale
Filled all the desert with inviolable voice
And still she cried, and still the world pursues,
'Jug Jug' to dirty ears.
And other withered stumps of time
Were told upon the walls; staring forms
Leaned out, leaning, hushing the room enclosed.
Footsteps shuffled on the stair.
Under the firelight, under the brush, her hair
Spread out in fiery points
Glowed into words, then would be savagely still.

'My nerves are bad to-night. Yes, bad. Stay with me.
'Speak to me. Why do you never speak. Speak.
     'What are you thinking of? What thinking? What?
'I never know what you are thinking. Think.'

I think we are in rats' alley
Where the dead men lost their bones.

'What is that noise?'

        The wind under the door.

'What is that noise now? What is the wind doing?'

        Nothing again nothing.

                        'Do

'You know nothing? Do you see nothing? Do you remember

'Nothing?'

    I remember

Those are pearls that were his eyes.

'Are you alive, or not? Is there nothing in your head?'

                          But

O O O O that Shakespeherian Rag—

It's so elegant

So intelligent

'What shall I do now? What shall I do?'

'I shall rush out as I am, and walk the street

'With my hair down, so. What shall we do tomorrow?

'What shall we ever do?'

             The hot water at ten.

And if it rains, a closed car at four.

And we shall play a game of chess,

Pressing lidless eyes and waiting for a knock upon the door.

When Lil's husband got demobbed, I said—
I didn't mince my words, I said to her myself,
Hurry up please its time
Now Albert's coming back, make yourself a bit smart.
He'll want to know what you done with that money he gave
   you
To get yourself some teeth. He did, I was there.
You have them all out, Lil, and get a nice set,
He said, I swear, I can't bear to look at you.
And no more can't I, I said, and think of poor Albert,
He's been in the army four years, he wants a good time,
And if you don't give it him, there's others will, I said.
Oh is there, she said. Something o' that, I said.
Then I'll know who to thank, she said, and give me a straight
   look.
Hurry up please its time
If you don't like it you can get on with it, I said.
Others can pick and choose if you can't.
But if Albert makes off, it won't be for lack of telling.
You ought to be ashamed, I said, to look so antique.
(And her only thirty-one.)

I can't help it, she said, pulling a long face,
It's them pills I took, to bring it off, she said.
(She's had five already, and nearly died of young George.)
The chemist said it would be all right, but I've never been
    the same.
You *are* a proper fool, I said.
Well, if Albert won't leave you alone, there it is, I said,
What you get married for if you don't want children?
Hurry up please its time
Well, that Sunday Albert was home, they had a hot gammon,
And they asked me in to dinner, to get the beauty of it hot—
Hurry up please its time
Hurry up please its time
Goonight Bill. Goonight Lou. Goonight May. Goonight.
Ta ta. Goonight. Goonight.
Good night, ladies, good night, sweet ladies, good night,
    good night.

III. The Fire Sermon

The river's tent is broken; the last fingers of leaf
Clutch and sink into the wet bank. The wind
Crosses the brown land, unheard. The nymphs are departed.
Sweet Thames, run softly, till I end my song.
The river bears no empty bottles, sandwich papers,
Silk handkerchiefs, cardboard boxes, cigarette ends
Or other testimony of summer nights. The nymphs are
  departed.
And their friends, the loitering heirs of City directors;
Departed, have left no addresses.
By the waters of Leman I sat down and wept . . .
Sweet Thames, run softly till I end my song,
Sweet Thames, run softly, for I speak not loud or long.
But at my back in a cold blast I hear
The rattle of the bones, and chuckle spread from ear to ear.

A rat crept softly through the vegetation
Dragging its slimy belly on the bank
While I was fishing in the dull canal
On a winter evening round behind the gashouse
Musing upon the king my brother's wreck
And on the king my father's death before him.

White bodies naked on the low damp ground
And bones cast in a little low dry garret,
Rattled by the rat's foot only, year to year.
But at my back from time to time I hear
The sound of horns and motors, which shall bring
Sweeney to Mrs. Porter in the spring.
O the moon shone bright on Mrs. Porter
And on her daughter
They wash their feet in soda water
Et O ces voix d'enfants, chantant dans la coupole!

Twit twit twit
Jug jug jug jug jug jug
So rudely forc'd.
Tereu

Unreal City
Under the brown fog of a winter noon
Mr. Eugenides, the Smyrna merchant
Unshaven, with a pocket full of currants
C.i.f. London: documents at sight,
Asked me in demotic French
To luncheon at the Cannon Street Hotel
Followed by a weekend at the Metropole.

At the violet hour, when the eyes and back
Turn upward from the desk, when the human engine waits
Like a taxi throbbing waiting,
I Tiresias, though blind, throbbing between two lives,
Old man with wrinkled female breasts, can see
At the violet hour, the evening hour that strives
Homeward, and brings the sailor home from sea,
The typist home at teatime, clears her breakfast, lights
Her stove, and lays out food in tins.
Out of the window perilously spread
Her drying combinations touched by the sun's last rays,
On the divan are piled (at night her bed)
Stockings, slippers, camisoles, and stays.
I Tiresias, old man with wrinkled dugs
Perceived the scene, and foretold the rest—
I too awaited the expected guest.
He, the young man carbuncular, arrives,
A small house agent's clerk, with one bold stare,
One of the low on whom assurance sits
As a silk hat on a Bradford millionaire.
The time is now propitious, as he guesses,
The meal is ended, she is bored and tired,
Endeavours to engage her in caresses
Which still are unreproved, if undesired.

Flushed and decided, he assaults at once;
Exploring hands encounter no defence;
His vanity requires no response,
And makes a welcome of indifference.
(And I Tiresias have foresuffered all
Enacted on this same divan or bed;
I who have sat by Thebes below the wall
And walked among the lowest of the dead.)
Bestows one final patronising kiss,
And gropes his way, finding the stairs unlit . . .

She turns and looks a moment in the glass,
Hardly aware of her departed lover;
Her brain allows one half-formed thought to pass:
'Well now that's done: and I'm glad it's over.'
When lovely woman stoops to folly and
Paces about her room again, alone,
She smooths her hair with automatic hand,
And puts a record on the gramophone.

'This music crept by me upon the waters'
And along the Strand, up Queen Victoria Street.
O City city, I can sometimes hear
Beside a public bar in Lower Thames Street,

The pleasant whining of a mandoline
And a clatter and a chatter from within
Where fishmen lounge at noon: where the walls
Of Magnus Martyr hold
Inexplicable splendour of Ionian white and gold.

          The river sweats
          Oil and tar
          The barges drift
          With the turning tide
          Red sails
          Wide
          To leeward, swing on the heavy spar.
          The barges wash
          Drifting logs
          Down Greenwich reach
          Past the Isle of Dogs.
                    Weialala leia
                    Wallala leialala

          Elizabeth and Leicester
          Beating oars
          The stern was formed
          A gilded shell

Red and gold
The brisk swell
Rippled both shores
Southwest wind
Carried down stream
The peal of bells
White towers
              Weialala leia
              Wallala leialala

'Trams and dusty trees.
Highbury bore me. Richmond and Kew
Undid me. By Richmond I raised my knees
Supine on the floor of a narrow canoe.'

'My feet are at Moorgate, and my heart
Under my feet. After the event
He wept. He promised "a new start."
I made no comment. What should I resent?'

'On Margate Sands.
I can connect
Nothing with nothing.
The broken fingernails of dirty hands.

My people humble people who expect
Nothing.'

        la la

To Carthage then I came

Burning burning burning burning
O Lord Thou pluckest me out
O Lord Thou pluckest

burning

IV. Death by Water

Phlebas the Phoenician, a fortnight dead,
Forgot the cry of gulls, and the deep sea swell
And the profit and loss.
                  A current under sea
Picked his bones in whispers. As he rose and fell
He passed the stages of his age and youth
Entering the whirlpool.
                Gentile or Jew
O you who turn the wheel and look to windward,
Consider Phlebas, who was once handsome and tall as
    you.

V. What the Thunder Said

After the torchlight red on sweaty faces
After the frosty silence in the gardens
After the agony in stony places
The shouting and the crying
Prison and palace and reverberation
Of thunder of spring over distant mountains
He who was living is now dead
We who were living are now dying
With a little patience

Here is no water but only rock
Rock and no water and the sandy road
The road winding above among the mountains
Which are mountains of rock without water
If there were water we should stop and drink
Amongst the rock one cannot stop or think
Sweat is dry and feet are in the sand
If there were only water amongst the rock
Dead mountain mouth of carious teeth that cannot spit
Here one can neither stand nor lie nor sit
There is not even silence in the mountains
But dry sterile thunder without rain
There is not even solitude in the mountains

But red sullen faces sneer and snarl
From doors of mudcracked houses
                              If there were water

   And no rock
   If there were rock
   And also water
   And water
   A spring
   A pool among the rock
   If there were the sound of water only
   Not the cicada
   And dry grass singing
   But sound of water over a rock
   Where the hermit-thrush sings in the pine trees
   Drip drop drip drop drop drop drop
   But there is no water

Who is the third who walks always beside you?
When I count, there are only you and I together
But when I look ahead up the white road
There is always another one walking beside you
Gliding wrapt in a brown mantle, hooded
I do not know whether a man or a woman
—But who is that on the other side of you?

What is that sound high in the air
Murmur of maternal lamentation
Who are those hooded hordes swarming
Over endless plains, stumbling in cracked earth
Ringed by the flat horizon only
What is the city over the mountains
Cracks and reforms and bursts in the violet air
Falling towers
Jerusalem Athens Alexandria
Vienna London
Unreal

A woman drew her long black hair out tight
And fiddled whisper music on those strings
And bats with baby faces in the violet light
Whistled, and beat their wings
And crawled head downward down a blackened wall
And upside down in air were towers
Tolling reminiscent bells, that kept the hours
And voices singing out of empty cisterns and exhausted wells

In this decayed hole among the mountains
In the faint moonlight, the grass is singing
Over the tumbled graves, about the chapel

There is the empty chapel, only the wind's home.
It has no windows, and the door swings,
Dry bones can harm no one.
Only a cock stood on the rooftree
Co co rico co co rico
In a flash of lightning. Then a damp gust
Bringing rain

Ganga was sunken, and the limp leaves
Waited for rain, while the black clouds
Gathered far distant, over Himavant.
The jungle crouched, humped in silence.
Then spoke the thunder
D<small>A</small>
Datta: what have we given?
My friend, blood shaking my heart
The awful daring of a moment's surrender
Which an age of prudence can never retract
By this, and this only, we have existed
Which is not to be found in our obituaries
Or in memories draped by the beneficent spider
Or under seals broken by the lean solicitor
In our empty rooms
D<small>A</small>

Dayadhvam: I have heard the key
Turn in the door once and turn once only
We think of the key, each in his prison
Thinking of the key, each confirms a prison
Only at nightfall, aethereal rumours
Revive for a moment a broken Coriolanus
Dᴀ
Damyata: The boat responded
Gaily, to the hand expert with sail and oar
The sea was calm, your heart would have responded
Gaily, when invited, beating obedient
To controlling hands

                      I sat upon the shore
Fishing, with the arid plain behind me
Shall I at least set my lands in order?
London Bridge is falling down falling down falling down
Poi s'ascose nel foco che gli affina
Quando fiam uti chelidon—O swallow swallow
Le Prince d'Aquitaine à la tour abolie
These fragments I have shored against my ruins
Why then Ile fit you. Hieronymo's mad againe.
Datta. Dayadhvam. Damyata.
                Shantih   shantih   shantih

THE HOLLOW MEN

A penny for the Old Guy

I

We are the hollow men
We are the stuffed men
Leaning together
Headpiece filled with straw. Alas!
Our dried voices, when
We whisper together
Are quiet and meaningless
As wind in dry grass
Or rats' feet over broken glass
In our dry cellar

Shape without form, shade without colour,
Paralysed force, gesture without motion;

Those who have crossed
With direct eyes, to death's other Kingdom
Remember us—if at all—not as lost
Violent souls, but only
As the hollow men
The stuffed men.

II

Eyes I dare not meet in dreams
In death's dream kingdom
These do not appear:
There, the eyes are
Sunlight on a broken column
There, is a tree swinging
And voices are
In the wind's singing
More distant and more solemn
Than a fading star.

Let me be no nearer
In death's dream kingdom
Let me also wear
Such deliberate disguises
Rat's coat, crowskin, crossed staves
In a field
Behaving as the wind behaves
No nearer—

Not that final meeting
In the twilight kingdom

III

This is the dead land
This is cactus land
Here the stone images
Are raised, here they receive
The supplication of a dead man's hand
Under the twinkle of a fading star.

Is it like this
In death's other kingdom
Waking alone
At the hour when we are
Trembling with tenderness
Lips that would kiss
Form prayers to broken stone.

IV

The eyes are not here
There are no eyes here
In this valley of dying stars
In this hollow valley
This broken jaw of our lost kingdoms

In this last of meeting places
We grope together
And avoid speech
Gathered on this beach of the tumid river

Sightless, unless
The eyes reappear
As the perpetual star
Multifoliate rose
Of death's twilight kingdom
The hope only
Of empty men.

V

Here we go round the prickly pear
Prickly pear prickly pear
Here we go round the prickly pear
At five o'clock in the morning.

Between the idea
And the reality
Between the motion
And the act
Falls the Shadow

For Thine is the Kingdom

Between the conception
And the creation
Between the emotion
And the response
Falls the Shadow

Life is very long

Between the desire
And the spasm
Between the potency
And the existence
Between the essence
And the descent
Falls the Shadow

                        For Thine is the Kingdom

For Thine is
Life is
For Thine is the

This is the way the world ends
This is the way the world ends
This is the way the world ends
Not with a bang but a whimper.

ASH-WEDNESDAY

I

Because I do not hope to turn again
Because I do not hope
Because I do not hope to turn
Desiring this man's gift and that man's scope
I no longer strive to strive towards such things
(Why should the agèd eagle stretch its wings?)
Why should I mourn
The vanished power of the usual reign?

Because I do not hope to know again
The infirm glory of the positive hour
Because I do not think
Because I know I shall not know
The one veritable transitory power
Because I cannot drink
There, where trees flower, and springs flow, for there is
      nothing again

Because I know that time is always time
And place is always and only place
And what is actual is actual only for one time
And only for one place
I rejoice that things are as they are and
I renounce the blessèd face
And renounce the voice
Because I cannot hope to turn again
Consequently I rejoice, having to construct something
Upon which to rejoice

And pray to God to have mercy upon us
And I pray that I may forget
These matters that with myself I too much discuss
Too much explain
Because I do not hope to turn again
Let these words answer
For what is done, not to be done again
May the judgement not be too heavy upon us

Because these wings are no longer wings to fly
But merely vans to beat the air
The air which is now thoroughly small and dry
Smaller and dryer than the will
Teach us to care and not to care
Teach us to sit still.

Pray for us sinners now and at the hour of our death
Pray for us now and at the hour of our death.

II

Lady, three white leopards sat under a juniper-tree
In the cool of the day, having fed to satiety
On my legs my heart my liver and that which had been
      contained
In the hollow round of my skull. And God said
Shall these bones live? shall these
Bones live? And that which had been contained
In the bones (which were already dry) said chirping:
Because of the goodness of this Lady
And because of her loveliness, and because
She honours the Virgin in meditation,
We shine with brightness. And I who am here dissembled
Proffer my deeds to oblivion, and my love
To the posterity of the desert and the fruit of the gourd.
It is this which recovers
My guts the strings of my eyes and the indigestible portions
Which the leopards reject. The Lady is withdrawn
In a white gown, to contemplation, in a white gown.
Let the whiteness of bones atone to forgetfulness.
There is no life in them. As I am forgotten
And would be forgotten, so I would forget
Thus devoted, concentrated in purpose. And God said

Prophesy to the wind, to the wind only for only
The wind will listen. And the bones sang chirping
With the burden of the grasshopper, saying

Lady of silences
Calm and distressed
Torn and most whole
Rose of memory
Rose of forgetfulness
Exhausted and life-giving
Worried reposeful
The single Rose
Is now the Garden
Where all loves end
Terminate torment
Of love unsatisfied
The greater torment
Of love satisfied
End of the endless
Journey to no end
Conclusion of all that
Is inconclusible
Speech without word and
Word of no speech

Grace to the Mother
For the Garden
Where all love ends.

Under a juniper-tree the bones sang, scattered and shining
We are glad to be scattered, we did little good to each other,
Under a tree in the cool of the day, with the blessing of sand,
Forgetting themselves and each other, united
In the quiet of the desert. This is the land which ye
Shall divide by lot. And neither division nor unity
Matters. This is the land. We have our inheritance.

III

At the first turning of the second stair
I turned and saw below
The same shape twisted on the banister
Under the vapour in the fetid air
Struggling with the devil of the stairs who wears
The deceitful face of hope and of despair.

At the second turning of the second stair
I left them twisting, turning below;
There were no more faces and the stair was dark,
Damp, jaggèd, like an old man's mouth drivelling, beyond
    repair,
Or the toothed gullet of an agèd shark.

At the first turning of the third stair
Was a slotted window bellied like the fig's fruit
And beyond the hawthorn blossom and a pasture scene
The broadbacked figure drest in blue and green
Enchanted the maytime with an antique flute.
Blown hair is sweet, brown hair over the mouth blown,
Lilac and brown hair;

Distraction, music of the flute, stops and steps of the mind
    over the third stair,
Fading, fading; strength beyond hope and despair
Climbing the third stair.

Lord, I am not worthy
Lord, I am not worthy

      but speak the word only.

IV

Who walked between the violet and the violet
Who walked between
The various ranks of varied green
Going in white and blue, in Mary's colour,
Talking of trivial things
In ignorance and in knowledge of eternal dolour
Who moved among the others as they walked,
Who then made strong the fountains and made fresh the
    springs

Made cool the dry rock and made firm the sand
In blue of larkspur, blue of Mary's colour,
Sovegna vos

Here are the years that walk between, bearing
Away the fiddles and the flutes, restoring
One who moves in the time between sleep and waking,
    wearing

White light folded, sheathed about her, folded.
The new years walk, restoring
Through a bright cloud of tears, the years, restoring
With a new verse the ancient rhyme. Redeem
The time. Redeem
The unread vision in the higher dream
While jewelled unicorns draw by the gilded hearse.

The silent sister veiled in white and blue
Between the yews, behind the garden god,
Whose flute is breathless, bent her head and signed but
    spoke no word

But the fountain sprang up and the bird sang down
Redeem the time, redeem the dream
The token of the word unheard, unspoken

Till the wind shake a thousand whispers from the yew

And after this our exile

V

If the lost word is lost, if the spent word is spent
If the unheard, unspoken
Word is unspoken, unheard;
Still is the unspoken word, the Word unheard,
The Word without a word, the Word within
The world and for the world;
And the light shone in darkness and
Against the Word the unstilled world still whirled
About the centre of the silent Word.

O my people, what have I done unto thee.

Where shall the word be found, where will the word
Resound? Not here, there is not enough silence
Not on the sea or on the islands, not
On the mainland, in the desert or the rain land,
For those who walk in darkness
Both in the day time and in the night time
The right time and the right place are not here
No place of grace for those who avoid the face
No time to rejoice for those who walk among noise and
    deny the voice

Will the veiled sister pray for
Those who walk in darkness, who chose thee and oppose thee,
Those who are torn on the horn between season and season,
    time and time, between
Hour and hour, word and word, power and power, those
    who wait
In darkness? Will the veiled sister pray
For children at the gate
Who will not go away and cannot pray:
Pray for those who chose and oppose

    O my people, what have I done unto thee.

Will the veiled sister between the slender
Yew trees pray for those who offend her
And are terrified and cannot surrender
And affirm before the world and deny between the rocks
In the last desert between the last blue rocks
The desert in the garden the garden in the desert
Of drouth, spitting from the mouth the withered apple-seed.

    O my people.

VI

Although I do not hope to turn again
Although I do not hope
Although I do not hope to turn

Wavering between the profit and the loss
In this brief transit where the dreams cross
The dreamcrossed twilight between birth and dying
(Bless me father) though I do not wish to wish these things
From the wide window towards the granite shore
The white sails still fly seaward, seaward flying
Unbroken wings

And the lost heart stiffens and rejoices
In the lost lilac and the lost sea voices
And the weak spirit quickens to rebel
For the bent golden-rod and the lost sea smell
Quickens to recover
The cry of quail and the whirling plover
And the blind eye creates
The empty forms between the ivory gates
And smell renews the salt savour of the sandy earth

This is the time of tension between dying and birth
The place of solitude where three dreams cross
Between blue rocks
But when the voices shaken from the yew-tree drift away
Let the other yew be shaken and reply.
Blessèd sister, holy mother, spirit of the fountain, spirit of
    the garden,
Suffer us not to mock ourselves with falsehood
Teach us to care and not to care
Teach us to sit still
Even among these rocks,
Our peace in His will
And even among these rocks
Sister, mother
And spirit of the river, spirit of the sea,
Suffer me not to be separated

And let my cry come unto Thee.

JOURNEY OF THE MAGI

'A cold coming we had of it,
Just the worst time of the year
For a journey, and such a long journey:
The ways deep and the weather sharp,
The very dead of winter.'
And the camels galled, sore-footed, refractory,
Lying down in the melting snow.
There were times we regretted
The summer palaces on slopes, the terraces,
And the silken girls bringing sherbet.
Then the camel men cursing and grumbling
And running away, and wanting their liquor and women,
And the night-fires going out, and the lack of shelters,
And the cities hostile and the towns unfriendly
And the villages dirty and charging high prices:
A hard time we had of it.
At the end we preferred to travel all night,
Sleeping in snatches,
With the voices singing in our ears, saying
That this was all folly.

Then at dawn we came down to a temperate valley,
Wet, below the snow line, smelling of vegetation,
With a running stream and a water-mill beating the darkness,
And three trees on the low sky.
And an old white horse galloped away in the meadow.
Then we came to a tavern with vine-leaves over the lintel,
Six hands at an open door dicing for pieces of silver,
And feet kicking the empty wine-skins.
But there was no information, and so we continued
And arrived at evening, not a moment too soon
Finding the place; it was (you may say) satisfactory.

All this was a long time ago, I remember,
And I would do it again, but set down
This set down
This: were we led all that way for
Birth or Death? There was a Birth, certainly,
We had evidence and no doubt. I had seen birth and death,
But had thought they were different; this Birth was
Hard and bitter agony for us, like Death, our death.
We returned to our places, these Kingdoms,
But no longer at ease here, in the old dispensation,
With an alien people clutching their gods.
I should be glad of another death.

MARINA

*Quis hic locus, quae
regio, quae mundi plaga?*

What seas what shores what grey rocks and what islands
What water lapping the bow
And scent of pine and the woodthrush singing through the
    fog
What images return
O my daughter.

Those who sharpen the tooth of the dog, meaning
Death
Those who glitter with the glory of the hummingbird,
    meaning
Death
Those who sit in the sty of contentment, meaning
Death
Those who suffer ecstasy of the animals, meaning
Death

Are become unsubstantial, reduced by a wind,
A breath of pine, and the woodsong fog
By this grace dissolved in place

What is this face, less clear and clearer
The pulse in the arm, less strong and stronger—
Given or lent? more distant than stars and nearer than the eye

Whispers and small laughter between leaves and hurrying feet
Under sleep, where all the waters meet.

Bowsprit cracked with ice and paint cracked with heat.
I made this, I have forgotten
And remember.
The rigging weak and the canvas rotten
Between one June and another September.
Made this unknowing, half conscious, unknown, my own.
The garboard strake leaks, the seams need caulking.
This form, this face, this life
Living to live in a world of time beyond me; let me
Resign my life for this life, my speech for that unspoken.
The awakened, lips parted, the hope, the new ships.

What seas what shores what granite islands towards my
   timbers
And woodthrush calling through the fog
My daughter.

CORIOLAN

I. Triumphal March

Stone, bronze, stone, steel, stone, oakleaves, horses' heels
Over the paving.
And the flags. And the trumpets. And so many eagles.
How many? Count them. And such a press of people.
We hardly knew ourselves that day, or knew the City.
This is the way to the temple, and we so many crowding the
    way.
So many waiting, how many waiting? what did it matter, on
    such a day?
Are they coming? No, not yet. You can see some eagles.
    And hear the trumpets.
Here they come. Is he coming?
The natural wakeful life of our Ego is a perceiving.
We can wait with our stools and our sausages.
What comes first? Can you see? Tell us. It is

    5,800,000 rifles and carbines,
      102,000 machine guns,
       28,000 trench mortars,
       53,000 field and heavy guns,

I cannot tell how many projectiles, mines and fuses,

    13,000 aeroplanes,

    24,000 aeroplane engines,

    50,000 ammunition waggons,

  now 55,000 army waggons,

    11,000 field kitchens,

     1,150 field bakeries.

What a time that took. Will it be he now? No,
Those are the golf club Captains, these the Scouts,
And now the *société gymnastique de Poissy*
And now come the Mayor and the Liverymen. Look
There he is now, look:
There is no interrogation in his eyes
Or in the hands, quiet over the horse's neck,
And the eyes watchful, waiting, perceiving, indifferent.
O hidden under the dove's wing, hidden in the turtle's breast,
Under the palmtree at noon, under the running water
At the still point of the turning world. O hidden.

Now they go up to the temple. Then the sacrifice.
Now come the virgins bearing urns, urns containing
Dust
Dust
Dust of dust, and now
Stone, bronze, stone, steel, stone, oakleaves, horses' heels
Over the paving.

That is all we could see. But how many eagles! and how many
    trumpets!
(And Easter Day, we didn't get to the country,
So we took young Cyril to church. And they rang a bell
And he said right out loud, *crumpets*.)
              Don't throw away that sausage,
It'll come in handy. He's artful. Please, will you
Give us a light?
Light
Light
Et les soldats faisaient la haie? ILS LA FAISAIENT.

II. Difficulties of a Statesman

CRY what shall I cry?
All flesh is grass: comprehending
The Companions of the Bath, the Knights of the British
    Empire, the Cavaliers,
O Cavaliers! of the Legion of Honour,
The Order of the Black Eagle (1st and 2nd class),
And the Order of the Rising Sun.
Cry cry what shall I cry?
The first thing to do is to form the committees:
The consultative councils, the standing committees, select
    committees and sub-committees.
One secretary will do for several committees.
What shall I cry?
Arthur Edward Cyril Parker is appointed telephone operator
At a salary of one pound ten a week rising by annual
    increments of five shillings
To two pounds ten a week; with a bonus of thirty shillings
    at Christmas
And one week's leave a year.
A committee has been appointed to nominate a commission
    of engineers
To consider the Water Supply.

A commission is appointed

For Public Works, chiefly the question of rebuilding the
    fortifications.

A commission is appointed

To confer with a Volscian commission

About perpetual peace: the fletchers and javelin-makers and
    smiths

Have appointed a joint committee to protest against the
    reduction of orders.

Meanwhile the guards shake dice on the marches

And the frogs (O Mantuan) croak in the marshes.

Fireflies flare against the faint sheet lightning

What shall I cry?

Mother mother

Here is the row of family portraits, dingy busts, all looking
    remarkably Roman,

Remarkably like each other, lit up successively by the flare

Of a sweaty torchbearer, yawning.

O hidden under the . . . Hidden under the . . . Where the
    dove's foot rested and locked for a moment,

A still moment, repose of noon, set under the upper branches
    of noon's widest tree

Under the breast feather stirred by the small wind after noon

There the cyclamen spreads its wings, there the clematis
    droops over the lintel
O mother (not among these busts, all correctly inscribed)
I a tired head among these heads
Necks strong to bear them
Noses strong to break the wind
Mother
May we not be some time, almost now, together,
If the mactations, immolations, oblations, impetrations,
Are now observed
May we not be
O hidden
Hidden in the stillness of noon, in the silent croaking night.
Come with the sweep of the little bat's wing, with the small
    flare of the firefly or lightning bug,
'Rising and falling, crowned with dust,' the small creatures,
The small creatures chirp thinly through the dust, through
    the night.
O mother
What shall I cry?
We demand a committee, a representative committee, a
    committee of investigation
            RESIGN   RESIGN   RESIGN

CHORUSES FROM "THE ROCK"

I

The Eagle soars in the summit of Heaven,
The Hunter with his dogs pursues his circuit.
O perpetual revolution of configured stars,
O perpetual recurrence of determined seasons,
O world of spring and autumn, birth and dying!
The endless cycle of idea and action,
Endless invention, endless experiment,
Brings knowledge of motion, but not of stillness;
Knowledge of speech, but not of silence;
Knowledge of words, and ignorance of the Word.
All our knowledge brings us nearer to our ignorance,
All our ignorance brings us nearer to death,
But nearness to death no nearer to GOD.
Where is the Life we have lost in living?
Where is the wisdom we have lost in knowledge?
Where is the knowledge we have lost in information?
The cycles of Heaven in twenty centuries
Bring us farther from GOD and nearer to the Dust.

I journeyed to London, to the timekept City,
Where the River flows, with foreign flotations.
There I was told: we have too many churches,
And too few chop-houses. There I was told:
Let the vicars retire. Men do not need the Church
In the place where they work, but where they spend their
    Sundays.
In the City, we need no bells:
Let them waken the suburbs.
I journeyed to the suburbs, and there I was told:
We toil for six days, on the seventh we must motor
To Hindhead, or Maidenhead.
If the weather is foul we stay at home and read the papers.
In industrial districts, there I was told
Of economic laws.
In the pleasant countryside, there it seemed
That the country now is only fit for picnics.
And the Church does not seem to be wanted
In country or in suburb; and in the town
Only for important weddings.

Silence! and preserve respectful distance.
For I perceive approaching
The Rock. Who will perhaps answer our doubtings.
The Rock. The Watcher. The Stranger.
He who has seen what has happened
And who sees what is to happen.
The Witness. The Critic. The Stranger.
The God-shaken, in whom is the truth inborn.

Enter the ROCK, *led by a* BOY:

THE ROCK:

The lot of man is ceaseless labour,
Or ceaseless idleness, which is still harder,
Or irregular labour, which is not pleasant.
I have trodden the winepress alone, and I know
That it is hard to be really useful, resigning
The things that men count for happiness, seeking
The good deeds that lead to obscurity, accepting
With equal face those that bring ignominy,
The applause of all or the love of none.
All men are ready to invest their money

But most expect dividends.
I say to you: *Make perfect your will.*
I say: take no thought of the harvest,
But only of proper sowing.

The world turns and the world changes,
But one thing does not change.
In all of my years, one thing does not change.
However you disguise it, this thing does not change:
The perpetual struggle of Good and Evil.
Forgetful, you neglect your shrines and churches;
The men you are in these times deride
What has been done of good, you find explanations
To satisfy the rational and enlightened mind.
Second, you neglect and belittle the desert.
The desert is not remote in southern tropics,
The desert is not only around the corner,
The desert is squeezed in the tube-train next to you,
The desert is in the heart of your brother.
The good man is the builder, if he build what is good.
I will show you the things that are now being done,

And some of the things that were long ago done,
That you may take heart. Make perfect your will.
Let me show you the work of the humble. Listen.

The lights fade; in the semi-darkness the voices of WORKMEN
are heard chanting.
In the vacant places
We will build with new bricks
There are hands and machines
And clay for new brick
And lime for new mortar
Where the bricks are fallen
We will build with new stone
Where the beams are rotten
We will build with new timbers
Where the word is unspoken
We will build with new speech
There is work together
A Church for all
And a job for each
Every man to his work.

Now a group of WORKMEN *is silhouetted against the*
dim sky. From farther away, they are answered by
voices of the UNEMPLOYED.
No man has hired us
With pocketed hands
And lowered faces
We stand about in open places
And shiver in unlit rooms.
Only the wind moves
Over empty fields, untilled
Where the plough rests, at an angle
To the furrow. In this land
There shall be one cigarette to two men,
To two women one half pint of bitter
Ale. In this land
No man has hired us.
Our life is unwelcome, our death
Unmentioned in 'The Times.'

Chant of WORKMEN *again.*
The river flows, the seasons turn
The sparrow and starling have no time to waste.
If men do not build
How shall they live?

When the field is tilled
And the wheat is bread
They shall not die in a shortened bed
And a narrow sheet. In this street
There is no beginning, no movement, no peace and no end
But noise without speech, food without taste.
Without delay, without haste
We would build the beginning and the end of this street.
We build the meaning:
A Church for all
And a job for each
Each man to his work.

III

The Word of the LORD came unto me, saying:
O miserable cities of designing men,
O wretched generation of enlightened men,
Betrayed in the mazes of your ingenuities,
Sold by the proceeds of your proper inventions:
I have given you hands which you turn from worship,
I have given you speech, for endless palaver,
I have given you my Law, and you set up commissions,
I have given you lips, to express friendly sentiments,
I have given you hearts, for reciprocal distrust.
I have given you power of choice, and you only alternate
Between futile speculation and unconsidered action.
Many are engaged in writing books and printing them,
Many desire to see their names in print,
Many read nothing but the race reports.
Much is your reading, but not the Word of GOD,
Much is your building, but not the House of GOD.
Will you build me a house of plaster, with corrugated roofing,
To be filled with a litter of Sunday newspapers?

1ST MALE VOICE:

A Cry from the East:
What shall be done to the shore of smoky ships?
Will you leave my people forgetful and forgotten
To idleness, labour, and delirious stupor?
There shall be left the broken chimney,
The peeled hull, a pile of rusty iron,
In a street of scattered brick where the goat climbs,
Where My Word is unspoken.

2ND MALE VOICE:

A Cry from the North, from the West and from the South
Whence thousands travel daily to the timekept City;
Where My Word is unspoken,
In the land of lobelias and tennis flannels
The rabbit shall burrow and the thorn revisit,
The nettle shall flourish on the gravel court,
And the wind shall say: 'Here were decent godless people:
Their only monument the asphalt road
And a thousand lost golf balls.'

We build in vain unless the LORD build with us.
Can you keep the City that the LORD keeps not with you?
A thousand policemen directing the traffic
Cannot tell you why you come or where you go.
A colony of cavies or a horde of active marmots
Build better than they that build without the LORD.
Shall we lift up our feet among perpetual ruins?
I have loved the beauty of Thy House, the peace of Thy sanctuary,
I have swept the floors and garnished the altars.
Where there is no temple there shall be no homes,
Though you have shelters and institutions,
Precarious lodgings while the rent is paid,
Subsiding basements where the rat breeds
Or sanitary dwellings with numbered doors
Or a house a little better than your neighbour's;
When the Stranger says: 'What is the meaning of this city?
Do you huddle close together because you love each other?'
What will you answer? 'We all dwell together
To make money from each other'? or 'This is a community'?
And the Stranger will depart and return to the desert.
O my soul, be prepared for the coming of the Stranger,
Be prepared for him who knows how to ask questions.

O weariness of men who turn from GOD
To the grandeur of your mind and the glory of your action,
To arts and inventions and daring enterprises,
To schemes of human greatness thoroughly discredited,
Binding the earth and the water to your service,
Exploiting the seas and developing the mountains,
Dividing the stars into common and preferred,
Engaged in devising the perfect refrigerator,
Engaged in working out a rational morality,
Engaged in printing as many books as possible,
Plotting of happiness and flinging empty bottles,
Turning from your vacancy to fevered enthusiasm
For nation or race or what you call humanity;
Though you forget the way to the Temple,
There is one who remembers the way to your door:
Life you may evade, but Death you shall not.
You shall not deny the Stranger.

IV

There are those who would build the Temple,
And those who prefer that the Temple should not be built.
In the days of Nehemiah the Prophet
There was no exception to the general rule.
In Shushan the palace, in the month Nisan,
He served the wine to the king Artaxerxes,
And he grieved for the broken city, Jerusalem;
And the King gave him leave to depart
That he might rebuild the city.
So he went, with a few, to Jerusalem,
And there, by the dragon's well, by the dung gate,
By the fountain gate, by the king's pool,
Jerusalem lay waste, consumed with fire;
No place for a beast to pass.
There were enemies without to destroy him,
And spies and self-seekers within,
When he and his men laid their hands to rebuilding the wall
So they built as men must build
With the sword in one hand and the trowel in the other.

VII

In the beginning GOD created the world. Waste and void.
Waste and void. And darkness was upon the face of
the deep.

And when there were men, in their various ways, they struggled
in torment towards GOD

Blindly and vainly, for man is a vain thing, and man with-
out GOD is a seed upon the wind: driven this way
and that, and finding no place of lodgement and ger-
mination.

They followed the light and the shadow, and the light led
them forward to light and the shadow led them to
darkness,

Worshipping snakes or trees, worshipping devils rather than
nothing: crying for life beyond life, for ecstasy not of the
flesh.

Waste and void. Waste and void. And darkness on the face
of the deep.

And the Spirit moved upon the face of the water.

And men who turned towards the light and were known of
the light

Invented the Higher Religions; and the Higher Religions were
good

And led men from light to light, to knowledge of Good and
    Evil.
But their light was ever surrounded and shot with darkness
As the air of temperate seas is pierced by the still dead breath of
    the Arctic Current;
And they came to an end, a dead end stirred with a flicker
    of life,
And they came to the withered ancient look of a child that
    has died of starvation.
Prayer wheels, worship of the dead, denial of this world,
    affirmation of rites with forgotten meanings
In the restless wind-whipped sand, or the hills where the wind
    will not let the snow rest.
Waste and void. Waste and void. And darkness on the face
    of the deep.

Then came, at a predetermined moment, a moment in time
    and of time,
A moment not out of time, but in time, in what we call history:
    transecting, bisecting the world of time, a moment in time
    but not like a moment of time,
A moment in time but time was made through that moment:
    for without the meaning there is no time, and that moment
    of time gave the meaning.

Then it seemed as if men must proceed from light to light, in the light of the Word,
Through the Passion and Sacrifice saved in spite of their negative being;
Bestial as always before, carnal, self-seeking as always before, selfish and purblind as ever before,
Yet always struggling, always reaffirming, always resuming their march on the way that was lit by the light;
Often halting, loitering, straying, delaying, returning, yet following no other way.

But it seems that something has happened that has never happened before: though we know not just when, or why, or how, or where.
Men have left GOD not for other gods, they say, but for no god; and this has never happened before
That men both deny gods and worship gods, professing first Reason,
And then Money, and Power, and what they call Life, or Race, or Dialectic.
The Church disowned, the tower overthrown, the bells upturned, what have we to do
But stand with empty hands and palms turned upwards
In an age which advances progressively backwards?

VOICE OF THE UNEMPLOYED (*afar off*):
          In this land
There shall be one cigarette to two men,
To two women one half pint of bitter
Ale. . . .

CHORUS:

What does the world say, does the whole world stray in
    high-powered cars on a by-pass way?

VOICE OF THE UNEMPLOYED (*more faintly*):
          In this land
No man has hired us. . . .

CHORUS:

Waste and void. Waste and void. And darkness on the face
    of the deep.
Has the Church failed mankind, or has mankind failed the
    Church?
When the Church is no longer regarded, not even opposed,
    and men have forgotten
All gods except Usury, Lust and Power.

OLD DEUTERONOMY

Old Deuteronomy's lived a long time;
    He's a Cat who has lived many lives in succession.
He was famous in proverb and famous in rhyme
    A long while before Queen Victoria's accession.
Old Deuteronomy's buried nine wives
    And more—I am tempted to say, ninety-nine;
And his numerous progeny prospers and thrives
    And the village is proud of him in his decline.
At the sight of that placid and bland physiognomy,
    When he sits in the sun on the vicarage wall,
The Oldest Inhabitant croaks: 'Well, of all . . .
    Things . . . Can it be . . . really! . . . No! . . . Yes! . . .
        Ho! hi!
        Oh, my eye!
My sight may be failing, but yet I confess
I believe it is Old Deuteronomy!'

Old Deuteronomy sits in the street,
     He sits in the High Street on market day;
The bullocks may bellow, the sheep they may bleat,
     But the dogs and the herdsmen will turn them away.
The cars and the lorries run over the kerb,
     And the villagers put up a notice: ROAD CLOSED—
So that nothing untoward may chance to disturb
     Deuteronomy's rest when he feels so disposed
Or when he's engaged in domestic economy:
     And the Oldest Inhabitant croaks: 'Well, of all . . .
     Things . . . Can it be . . . really! . . . No! . . . Yes! . . .
     Ho! hi!
     Oh, my eye!
I'm deaf of an ear now, but yet I can guess
That the cause of the trouble is Old Deuteronomy!'

Old Deuteronomy lies on the floor
     Of the Fox and French Horn for his afternoon sleep;
And when the men say: 'There's just time for one more,'
     Then the landlady from her back parlour will peep
And say: 'Now then, out you go, by the back door,
     For Old Deuteronomy mustn't be woken—

I'll have the police if there's any uproar'—

    And out they all shuffle, without a word spoken.

The digestive repose of that feline's gastronomy

    Must never be broken, whatever befall:

And the Oldest Inhabitant croaks: 'Well, of all . . .

    Things . . . Can it be . . . really! . . . Yes! . . . No! . . .

        Ho! hi!

        Oh, my eye!

My legs may be tottery, I must go slow

And be careful of Old Deuteronomy!'

SWEENEY AGONISTES

Fragments of an Aristophanic Melodrama

> *Orestes: You don't see them, you don't—but I see them;*
> *they are hunting me down, I must move on.*
> CHOEPHOROI.

> *Hence the soul cannot be possessed of the divine union,*
> *until it has divested itself of the love of created beings.*
> ST. JOHN OF THE CROSS.

Fragment of a Prologue

DUSTY.   DORIS.

DUSTY: How about Pereira?
DORIS: What about Pereira?
         I don't care.
DUSTY: You don't care!
         Who pays the rent?
DORIS: Yes he pays the rent
DUSTY: Well some men don't and some men do
         Some men don't and you know who
DORIS: You can have Pereira

DUSTY: What about Pereira?

DORIS: He's no gentleman, Pereira:

You can't trust him!

DUSTY: Well that's true.

He's no gentleman if you can't trust him

And *if* you can't trust him—

Then you never know what he's going to do.

DORIS: No it wouldn't do to be too nice to Pereira.

DUSTY: Now Sam's a gentleman through and through.

DORIS: I like Sam

DUSTY: *I* like Sam

Yes and Sam's a nice boy too.

He's a funny fellow

DORIS: He *is* a funny fellow

He's like a fellow once I knew.

He could make you laugh.

DUSTY: Sam can make you laugh:

Sam's all right

DORIS: But Pereira won't do.

We can't have Pereira

DUSTY: Well what you going to do?

TELEPHONE: Ting a ling ling

Ting a ling ling

DUSTY: That's Pereira

109

DORIS: Yes that's Pereira

DUSTY: Well what you going to do?

TELEPHONE: Ting a ling ling
                  Ting a ling ling

DUSTY: That's Pereira

DORIS: Well can't you stop that horrible noise?
        Pick up the receiver

DUSTY: What'll I say!

DORIS: Say what you like: say I'm ill,
        Say I broke my leg on the stairs
        Say we've had a fire

DUSTY: Hello Hello are you there?
        Yes this is Miss Dorrance's *flat*—
        Oh Mr. Pereira is that you? how do you do!
        Oh I'm *so* sorry. I *am* so sorry
        But Doris came home with a terrible chill
        No, just a chill
        Oh I *think* it's only a chill
        Yes indeed I hope so too—
        Well I *hope* we shan't have to call a doctor
        Doris just hates having a doctor
        She says will you ring up on Monday
        She hopes to be all right on Monday
        I say do you mind if I ring off now

She's got her feet in mustard and water
I said I'm giving her mustard and water
All right, Monday you'll phone through.
Yes I'll tell her. Good bye. Goooood bye.
I'm sure, that's very kind of *you*.

Ah-h-h

DORIS: Now I'm going to cut the cards for to-night.
Oh guess what the first is

DUSTY: First is. What is?

DORIS: The King of Clubs

DUSTY: That's Pereira

DORIS: It might be Sweeney

DUSTY: It's Pereira

DORIS: It might *just* as well be Sweeney

DUSTY: Well anyway it's very queer.

DORIS: Here's the four of diamonds, what's that
mean?

DUSTY (*reading*): 'A small sum of money, or a present
Of wearing apparel, or a party.'
That's queer too.

DORIS: Here's the three. What's that mean?

DUSTY: 'News of an absent friend.'—Pereira!

DORIS: The Queen of Hearts!—Mrs. Porter!

DUSTY: Or it might be you

111

DORIS: Or it might be you

We're all hearts. You can't be sure.

It just depends on what comes next.

You've got to *think* when you read the cards,

It's not a thing that anyone can do.

DUSTY: Yes I know you've a touch with the cards

What comes next?

DORIS: What comes next. It's the six.

DUSTY: 'A quarrel. An estrangement. Separation of friends.'

DORIS: Here's the two of spades.

DUSTY: The *two of spades*!

THAT'S THE COFFIN!!

DORIS: THAT'S THE COFFIN?

Oh good heavens what'll I do?

Just before a party too!

DUSTY: Well it needn't be yours, it may mean a friend.

DORIS: No it's mine. I'm sure it's mine.

I dreamt of weddings all last night.

Yes it's mine. I know it's mine.

Oh good heavens what'll I do.

Well I'm not going to draw any more,

You cut for luck. You cut for luck.

It might break the spell. You cut for luck.

DUSTY: The Knave of Spades.

DORIS: That'll be Snow

DUSTY: Or it might be Swarts

DORIS: Or it might be Snow

DUSTY: It's a funny thing how I draw court cards—

DORIS: There's a lot in the way you pick them up

DUSTY: There's an awful lot in the way you feel

DORIS: Sometimes they'll tell you nothing at all

DUSTY: You've got to know what you want to ask them

DORIS: You've got to know what you want to know

DUSTY: It's no use asking them too much

DORIS: It's no use asking more than once

DUSTY: Sometimes they're no use at all.

DORIS: I'd like to know about that coffin.

DUSTY: Well I never! What did I tell you?

Wasn't I saying I always draw court cards?

The Knave of Hearts!

(*Whistle outside of the window.*)

Well I *never*

What a co*in*cidence! Cards are queer!

(*Whistle again.*)

DORIS: Is that Sam?

DUSTY: Of course it's Sam!

DORIS: Of course, the Knave of Hearts *is* Sam!

DUSTY (*leaning out of the window*): Hello Sam!

WAUCHOPE:	Hello dear
	How many's up there?
DUSTY:	Nobody's up here
	How many's down there?
WAUCHOPE:	Four of us here.
	Wait till I put the car round the corner
	We'll be right up
DUSTY:	All right, come up.
DUSTY	(*to* DORIS): Cards are queer.
DORIS:	I'd like to know about that coffin.

KNOCK KNOCK KNOCK

KNOCK KNOCK KNOCK

KNOCK

KNOCK

KNOCK

DORIS. DUSTY. WAUCHOPE. HORSFALL.
KLIPSTEIN. KRUMPACKER.

WAUCHOPE: Hello Doris! Hello Dusty! How do you do!
How come? how come? will you permit me—
I think you girls both know Captain Horsfall—
We want you to meet two friends of ours,
American gentlemen here on business.
Meet Mr. Klipstein. Meet Mr. Krumpacker.

KLIPSTEIN: How do you do

KRUMPACKER: How do you do

KLIPSTEIN: I'm very pleased to make your acquaintance

KRUMPACKER: Extremely pleased to become acquainted

KLIPSTEIN: Sam—I should say Loot Sam Wauchope

KRUMPACKER: Of the Canadian Expeditionary Force—

KLIPSTEIN: The Loot has told us a lot about you.

KRUMPACKER: We were all in the war together

    Klip and me and the Cap and Sam.

KLIPSTEIN: Yes we did our bit, as you folks say,

      I'll tell the world we got the Hun on the run

KRUMPACKER: What about that poker game? eh what Sam?

    What about that poker game in Bordeaux?

    Yes Miss Dorrance you get Sam

    To tell about that poker game in Bordeaux.

DUSTY: Do you know London well, Mr. Krumpacker?

KLIPSTEIN: No we never been here before

KRUMPACKER: We hit this town last night for the first time

KLIPSTEIN: And I certainly hope it won't be the last time.

DORIS: You like London, Mr. Klipstein?

KRUMPACKER: Do we like London? do we like London!

    Do we like London!! Eh what Klip?

KLIPSTEIN: Say, Miss—er—uh—London's swell.

    We like London fine.

KRUMPACKER: Perfectly slick.

DUSTY: Why don't you come and live here then?

KLIPSTEIN: Well, no, Miss—er—you haven't quite got it
> (I'm afraid I didn't quite catch your name—
> But I'm very pleased to meet you all the same)—
> London's a little too gay for us
> Yes I'll say a little too gay.

KRUMPACKER: Yes London's a little too gay for us
> Don't think I mean anything *coarse*—
> But I'm afraid we couldn't stand the pace.
> What about it Klip?

KLIPSTEIN: You said it, Krum.
> London's a slick place, London's a swell place,
> London's a fine place to come on a visit—

KRUMPACKER: Specially when you got a real live Britisher
> A guy like Sam to show you around.
> Sam of course is at *home* in London,
> And he's promised to show us around.

Fragment of an Agon

SWEENEY. WAUCHOPE. HORSFALL. KLIPSTEIN.
KRUMPACKER. SWARTS. SNOW. DORIS. DUSTY.

SWEENEY: I'll carry you off
 To a cannibal isle.
DORIS: You'll be the cannibal!
SWEENEY: You'll be the missionary!
 You'll be my little seven stone missionary!
 I'll gobble you up. I'll be the cannibal.
DORIS: You'll carry me off? To a cannibal isle?
SWEENEY: I'll be the cannibal.
DORIS: I'll be the missionary.
 I'll convert you!
SWEENEY: I'll convert *you*!
 Into a stew.
 A nice little, white little, missionary stew.
DORIS: You wouldn't eat me!
SWEENEY: Yes I'd eat you!
 In a nice little, white little, soft little, tender little,
 Juicy little, right little, missionary stew.
 You see this egg
 You see this egg

Well that's life on a crocodile isle.

There's no telephones

There's no gramophones

There's no motor cars

No two-seaters, no six-seaters,

No Citroën, no Rolls-Royce.

Nothing to eat but the fruit as it grows.

Nothing to see but the palmtrees one way

And the sea the other way,

Nothing to hear but the sound of the surf.

Nothing at all but three things

DORIS: What things?

SWEENEY: Birth, and copulation, and death.

That's all, that's all, that's all, that's all,

Birth, and copulation, and death.

DORIS: I'd be bored.

SWEENEY: You'd be bored.

Birth, and copulation, and death.

DORIS: I'd be bored.

SWEENEY: You'd be bored.

Birth, and copulation, and death.

That's all the facts when you come to brass tacks:

Birth, and copulation, and death.

I've been born, and once is enough.

You dont remember, but I remember,
Once is enough.

SONG BY WAUCHOPE AND HORSFALL
SWARTS AS TAMBO. SNOW AS BONES

Under the bamboo
Bamboo bamboo
Under the bamboo tree
Two live as one
One live as two
Two live as three
Under the bam
Under the boo
Under the bamboo tree.

Where the breadfruit fall
And the penguin call
And the sound is the sound of the sea
Under the bam
Under the boo
Under the bamboo tree

Where the Gauguin maids
In the banyan shades
Wear palmleaf drapery
Under the bam
Under the boo
Under the bamboo tree.

Tell me in what part of the wood
Do you want to flirt with me?
Under the breadfruit, banyan, palmleaf
Or under the bamboo tree?
Any old tree will do for me
Any old wood is just as good
Any old isle is just my style
Any fresh egg
Any fresh egg
And the sound of the coral sea.

DORIS: I dont like eggs; I never liked eggs;
And I dont like life on your crocodile isle.

SONG BY KLIPSTEIN AND KRUMPACKER

SNOW AND SWARTS AS BEFORE

My little island girl
My little island girl
I'm going to stay with you
And we won't worry what to do
We won't have to catch any trains
And we won't go home when it rains
We'll gather hibiscus flowers
For it won't be minutes but hours
For it won't be hours but years

diminuendo {
And the morning
And the evening
And noontime
And night
Morning
Evening
Noontime
Night
}

DORIS: That's not life, that's no life

Why I'd just as soon be dead.

SWEENEY: That's what life is. Just is

DORIS: What is?

What's that life is?

SWEENEY: Life is death.

I knew a man once did a girl in—

DORIS: Oh Mr. Sweeney, please dont talk,

I cut the cards before you came

And I drew the coffin

SWARTS: *You* drew the coffin?

DORIS: I drew the COFFIN very last card.

I dont care for such conversation

A woman runs a terrible risk.

SNOW: Let Mr. Sweeney continue his story.

I assure you, Sir, we are very interested.

SWEENEY: I knew a man once did a girl in

Any man might do a girl in

Any man has to, needs to, wants to

Once in a lifetime, do a girl in.

Well he kept her there in a bath

With a gallon of lysol in a bath

SWARTS: These fellows always get pinched in the end.

SNOW: Excuse me, they dont all get pinched in the end.

What about them bones on Epsom Heath?

I seen that in the papers

You seen it in the papers

They *dont* all get pinched in the end.

DORIS: A woman runs a terrible risk.

SNOW: Let Mr. Sweeney continue his story.

SWEENEY: This one didn't get pinched in the end

But that's another story too.

This went on for a couple of months

Nobody came

And nobody went

But he took in the milk and he paid the rent.

SWARTS: What did he do?

All that time, what did he do?

SWEENEY: What did he do! what did he do?

That dont apply.

Talk to live men about what they do.

He used to come and see me sometimes

I'd give him a drink and cheer him up.

DORIS: Cheer him up?

DUSTY: Cheer him up?

SWEENEY: Well here again that dont apply
But I've gotta use words when I talk to you.
But here's what I was going to say.
He didn't know if he was alive
                and the girl was dead
He didn't know if the girl was alive
                and he was dead
He didn't know if they both were alive
                or both were dead
If he was alive then the milkman wasn't
                and the rent-collector wasn't
And if they were alive then he was dead.
There wasn't any joint
There wasn't any joint
For when you're alone
When you're alone like he was alone
You're either or neither
I tell you again it dont apply
Death or life or life or death
Death is life and life is death
I gotta use words when I talk to you
But if you understand or if you dont
That's nothing to me and nothing to you

We all gotta do what we gotta do
We're gona sit here and drink this booze
We're gona sit here and have a tune
We're gona stay and we're gona go
And somebody's gotta pay the rent
DORIS: I know who
SWEENEY: But that's nothing to me and nothing to you.

FULL CHORUS: WAUCHOPE, HORSFALL,
KLIPSTEIN, KRUMPACKER

When you're alone in the middle of the night and you
    wake in a sweat and a hell of a fright
When you're alone in the middle of the bed and you
    wake like someone hit you in the head
You've had a cream of a nightmare dream and you've
    got the hoo-ha's coming to you.
Hoo hoo hoo
You dreamt you waked up at seven o'clock and it's foggy
    and it's damp and it's dawn and it's dark
And you wait for a knock and the turning of a lock for
    you know the hangman's waiting for you.
And perhaps you're alive

And perhaps you're dead
Hoo ha ha
Hoo ha ha
Hoo
Hoo
Hoo
Knock Knock Knock
Knock Knock Knock
Knock
Knock
Knock

FROM *FOUR QUARTETS*

Burnt Norton

τοῦ λόγου δ' ἐόντος ξυνοῦ ζώουσιν οἱ πολλοί
ὡς ἰδίαν ἔχοντες φρόνησιν.

I. p. 77. Fr. 2.

ὁδὸς ἄνω κάτω μία καὶ ὡυτή.

I. p. 89. Fr. 60.

Diels: Die Fragmente der Vorsokratiker (Herakleitos).

I

Time present and time past
Are both perhaps present in time future,
And time future contained in time past.
If all time is eternally present
All time is unredeemable.
What might have been is an abstraction
Remaining a perpetual possibility
Only in a world of speculation.
What might have been and what has been
Point to one end, which is always present.
Footfalls echo in the memory

Down the passage which we did not take
Towards the door we never opened
Into the rose-garden. My words echo
Thus, in your mind.
                         But to what purpose
Disturbing the dust on a bowl of rose-leaves
I do not know.
                    Other echoes
Inhabit the garden. Shall we follow?
Quick, said the bird, find them, find them,
Round the corner. Through the first gate,
Into our first world, shall we follow
The deception of the thrush? Into our first world.
There they were, dignified, invisible,
Moving without pressure, over the dead leaves,
In the autumn heat, through the vibrant air,
And the bird called, in response to
The unheard music hidden in the shrubbery,
And the unseen eyebeam crossed, for the roses
Had the look of flowers that are looked at.
There they were as our guests, accepted and accepting.
So we moved, and they, in a formal pattern,
Along the empty alley, into the box circle,
To look down into the drained pool.

Dry the pool, dry concrete, brown edged,
And the pool was filled with water out of sunlight,
And the lotos rose, quietly, quietly,
The surface glittered out of heart of light,
And they were behind us, reflected in the pool.
Then a cloud passed, and the pool was empty.
Go, said the bird, for the leaves were full of children,
Hidden excitedly, containing laughter.
Go, go, go, said the bird: human kind
Cannot bear very much reality.
Time past and time future
What might have been and what has been
Point to one end, which is always present.

II

Garlic and sapphires in the mud
Clot the bedded axle-tree.
The trilling wire in the blood
Sings below inveterate scars
Appeasing long forgotten wars.
The dance along the artery
The circulation of the lymph
Are figured in the drift of stars
Ascend to summer in the tree
We move above the moving tree
In light upon the figured leaf
And hear upon the sodden floor
Below, the boarhound and the boar
Pursue their pattern as before
But reconciled among the stars.

At the still point of the turning world. Neither flesh nor
    fleshless;
Neither from nor towards; at the still point, there the
    dance is,
But neither arrest nor movement. And do not call it fixity,
Where past and future are gathered. Neither movement

from nor towards,
Neither ascent nor decline. Except for the point, the still
    point,
There would be no dance, and there is only the dance.
I can only say, *there* we have been: but I cannot say where.
And I cannot say, how long, for that is to place it in time.

The inner freedom from the practical desire,
The release from action and suffering, release from the
    inner
And the outer compulsion, yet surrounded
By a grace of sense, a white light still and moving,
Erhebung without motion, concentration
Without elimination, both a new world
And the old made explicit, understood
In the completion of its partial ecstasy,
The resolution of its partial horror.
Yet the enchainment of past and future
Woven in the weakness of the changing body,
Protects mankind from heaven and damnation
Which flesh cannot endure.
                        Time past and time future
Allow but a little consciousness.

To be conscious is not to be in time
But only in time can the moment in the rose-garden,
The moment in the arbour where the rain beat,
The moment in the draughty church at smokefall
Be remembered; involved with past and future.
Only through time time is conquered.

III

Here is a place of disaffection
Time before and time after
In a dim light: neither daylight
Investing form with lucid stillness
Turning shadow into transient beauty
With slow rotation suggesting permanence
Nor darkness to purify the soul
Emptying the sensual with deprivation
Cleansing affection from the temporal.
Neither plenitude nor vacancy. Only a flicker
Over the strained time-ridden faces
Distracted from distraction by distraction
Filled with fancies and empty of meaning
Tumid apathy with no concentration
Men and bits of paper, whirled by the cold wind
That blows before and after time,
Wind in and out of unwholesome lungs
Time before and time after.
Eructation of unhealthy souls
Into the faded air, the torpid
Driven on the wind that sweeps the gloomy hills of
     London,

Hampstead and Clerkenwell, Campden and Putney,
Highgate, Primrose and Ludgate. Not here
Not here the darkness, in this twittering world.

Descend lower, descend only
Into the world of perpetual solitude,
World not world, but that which is not world,
Internal darkness, deprivation
And destitution of all property,
Desiccation of the world of sense,
Evacuation of the world of fancy,
Inoperancy of the world of spirit;
This is the one way, and the other
Is the same, not in movement
But abstention from movement; while the world moves
In appetency, on its metalled ways
Of time past and time future.

IV

Time and the bell have buried the day,
The black cloud carries the sun away.
Will the sunflower turn to us, will the clematis
Stray down, bend to us; tendril and spray
Clutch and cling?
Chill
Fingers of yew be curled
Down on us? After the kingfisher's wing
Has answered light to light, and is silent, the light is still
At the still point of the turning world.

V

Words move, music moves
Only in time; but that which is only living
Can only die. Words, after speech, reach
Into the silence. Only by the form, the pattern,
Can words or music reach
The stillness, as a Chinese jar still
Moves perpetually in its stillness.
Not the stillness of the violin, while the note lasts,
Not that only, but the co-existence,
Or say that the end precedes the beginning,
And the end and the beginning were always there
Before the beginning and after the end.
And all is always now. Words strain,
Crack and sometimes break, under the burden,
Under the tension, slip, slide, perish,
Decay with imprecision, will not stay in place,
Will not stay still. Shrieking voices
Scolding, mocking, or merely chattering,
Always assail them. The Word in the desert
Is most attacked by voices of temptation,
The crying shadow in the funeral dance,
The loud lament of the disconsolate chimera.

The detail of the pattern is movement,
As in the figure of the ten stairs.
Desire itself is movement
Not in itself desirable;
Love is itself unmoving,
Only the cause and end of movement,
Timeless, and undesiring
Except in the aspect of time
Caught in the form of limitation
Between un-being and being.
Sudden in a shaft of sunlight
Even while the dust moves
There rises the hidden laughter
Of children in the foliage
Quick now, here, now, always—
Ridiculous the waste sad time
Stretching before and after.

Little Gidding

I

Midwinter spring is its own season
Sempiternal though sodden towards sundown,
Suspended in time, between pole and tropic.
When the short day is brightest, with frost and fire,
The brief sun flames the ice, on pond and ditches,
In windless cold that is the heart's heat,
Reflecting in a watery mirror
A glare that is blindness in the early afternoon.
And glow more intense than blaze of branch, or brazier,
Stirs the dumb spirit: no wind, but pentecostal fire
In the dark time of the year. Between melting and freezing
The soul's sap quivers. There is no earth smell
Or smell of living thing. This is the spring time
But not in time's covenant. Now the hedgerow
Is blanched for an hour with transitory blossom
Of snow, a bloom more sudden
Than that of summer, neither budding nor fading,
Not in the scheme of generation.
Where is the summer, the unimaginable
Zero summer?

If you came this way,
Taking the route you would be likely to take
From the place you would be likely to come from,
If you came this way in may time, you would find the
    hedges
White again, in May, with voluptuary sweetness.
It would be the same at the end of the journey,
If you came at night like a broken king,
If you came by day not knowing what you came for,
It would be the same, when you leave the rough road
And turn behind the pig-sty to the dull façade
And the tombstone. And what you thought you came for
Is only a shell, a husk of meaning
From which the purpose breaks only when it is fulfilled
If at all. Either you had no purpose
Or the purpose is beyond the end you figured
And is altered in fulfilment. There are other places
Which also are the world's end, some at the sea jaws,
Or over a dark lake, in a desert or a city—
But this is the nearest, in place and time,
Now and in England.

If you came this way,
Taking any route, starting from anywhere,

At any time or at any season,
It would always be the same: you would have to put off
Sense and notion. You are not here to verify,
Instruct yourself, or inform curiosity
Or carry report. You are here to kneel
Where prayer has been valid. And prayer is more
Than an order of words, the conscious occupation
Of the praying mind, or the sound of the voice praying.
And what the dead had no speech for, when living,
They can tell you, being dead: the communication
Of the dead is tongued with fire beyond the language of the
    living.
Here, the intersection of the timeless moment
Is England and nowhere. Never and always.

II

Ash on an old man's sleeve
Is all the ash the burnt roses leave.
Dust in the air suspended
Marks the place where a story ended.
Dust inbreathed was a house—
The wall, the wainscot and the mouse.
The death of hope and despair,
    This is the death of air.

There are flood and drouth
Over the eyes and in the mouth,
Dead water and dead sand
Contending for the upper hand.
The parched eviscerate soil
Gapes at the vanity of toil,
Laughs without mirth.
    This is the death of earth.

Water and fire succeed
The town, the pasture and the weed.
Water and fire deride
The sacrifice that we denied.

Water and fire shall rot
The marred foundations we forgot,
Of sanctuary and choir.
       This is the death of water and fire.

In the uncertain hour before the morning
       Near the ending of interminable night
       At the recurrent end of the unending
After the dark dove with the flickering tongue
       Had passed below the horizon of his homing
       While the dead leaves still rattled on like tin
Over the asphalt where no other sound was
       Between three districts whence the smoke arose
       I met one walking, loitering and hurried
As if blown towards me like the metal leaves
       Before the urban dawn wind unresisting.
       And as I fixed upon the down-turned face
That pointed scrutiny with which we challenge
       The first-met stranger in the waning dusk
       I caught the sudden look of some dead master
Whom I had known, forgotten, half recalled
       Both one and many; in the brown baked features
       The eyes of a familiar compound ghost
Both intimate and unidentifiable.

So I assumed a double part, and cried
And heard another's voice cry: 'What! are *you* here?'
Although we were not. I was still the same,
Knowing myself yet being someone other—
And he a face still forming; yet the words sufficed
To compel the recognition they preceded.
And so, compliant to the common wind,
Too strange to each other for misunderstanding,
In concord at this intersection time
Of meeting nowhere, no before and after,
We trod the pavement in a dead patrol
I said: 'The wonder that I feel is easy,
Yet ease is cause of wonder. Therefore speak:
I may not comprehend, may not remember.'
And he: 'I am not eager to rehearse
My thoughts and theory which you have forgotten.
These things have served their purpose: let them be.
So with your own, and pray they be forgiven
By others, as I pray you to forgive
Both bad and good. Last season's fruit is eaten
And the fullfed beast shall kick the empty pail.
For last year's words belong to last year's language
And next year's words await another voice.

But, as the passage now presents no hindrance
　　To the spirit unappeased and peregrine
　　Between two worlds become much like each other,
So I find words I never thought to speak
　　In streets I never thought I should revisit
　　When I left my body on a distant shore.
Since our concern was speech, and speech impelled us
　　To purify the dialect of the tribe
　　And urge the mind to aftersight and foresight,
Let me disclose the gifts reserved for age
　　To set a crown upon your lifetime's effort.
　　First, the cold friction of expiring sense
Without enchantment, offering no promise
　　But bitter tastelessness of shadow fruit
　　As body and soul begin to fall asunder.
Second, the conscious impotence of rage
　　At human folly, and the laceration
　　Of laughter at what ceases to amuse.
And last, the rending pain of re-enactment
　　Of all that you have done, and been; the shame
　　Of motives late revealed, and the awareness
Of things ill done and done to others' harm
　　Which once you took for exercise of virtue.
　　Then fools' approval stings, and honour stains.

From wrong to wrong the exasperated spirit
    Proceeds, unless restored by that refining fire
    Where you must move in measure, like a dancer.'
The day was breaking. In the disfigured street
    He left me, with a kind of valediction,
    And faded on the blowing of the horn.

III

There are three conditions which often look alike
Yet differ completely, flourish in the same hedgerow:
Attachment to self and to things and to persons, detachment
From self and from things and from persons; and, growing
    between them, indifference
Which resembles the others as death resembles life,
Being between two lives—unflowering, between
The live and the dead nettle. This is the use of memory:
For liberation—not less of love but expanding
Of love beyond desire, and so liberation
From the future as well as the past. Thus, love of a country
Begins as attachment to our own field of action
And comes to find that action of little importance
Though never indifferent. History may be servitude,
History may be freedom. See, now they vanish,
The faces and places, with the self which, as it could, loved
    them,
To become renewed, transfigured, in another pattern.

Sin is Behovely, but
All shall be well, and
All manner of thing shall be well.

If I think, again, of this place,
And of people, not wholly commendable,
Of no immediate kin or kindness,
But some of peculiar genius,
All touched by a common genius,
United in the strife which divided them;
If I think of a king at nightfall,
Of three men, and more, on the scaffold
And a few who died forgotten
In other places, here and abroad,
And of one who died blind and quiet,
Why should we celebrate
These dead men more than the dying?
It is not to ring the bell backward
Nor is it an incantation
To summon the spectre of a Rose.
We cannot revive old factions
We cannot restore old policies
Or follow an antique drum.
These men, and those who opposed them
And those whom they opposed
Accept the constitution of silence
And are folded in a single party.
Whatever we inherit from the fortunate

We have taken from the defeated
What they had to leave us—a symbol:
A symbol perfected in death.
And all shall be well and
All manner of thing shall be well
By the purification of the motive
In the ground of our beseeching.

IV

The dove descending breaks the air
With flame of incandescent terror
Of which the tongues declare
The one discharge from sin and error.
The only hope, or else despair
 Lies in the choice of pyre or pyre—
 To be redeemed from fire by fire.

Who then devised the torment? Love.
Love is the unfamiliar Name
Behind the hands that wove
The intolerable shirt of flame
Which human power cannot remove.
 We only live, only suspire
 Consumed by either fire or fire.

V

What we call the beginning is often the end
And to make an end is to make a beginning.
The end is where we start from. And every phrase
And sentence that is right (where every word is at home,
Taking its place to support the others,
The word neither diffident nor ostentatious,
An easy commerce of the old and the new,
The common word exact without vulgarity,
The formal word precise but not pedantic,
The complete consort dancing together)
Every phrase and every sentence is an end and a
    beginning,
Every poem an epitaph. And any action
Is a step to the block, to the fire, down the sea's throat
Or to an illegible stone: and that is where we start.
We die with the dying:
See, they depart, and we go with them.
We are born with the dead:
See, they return, and bring us with them.
The moment of the rose and the moment of the yew-tree
Are of equal duration. A people without history
Is not redeemed from time, for history is a pattern

Of timeless moments. So, while the light fails
On a winter's afternoon, in a secluded chapel
History is now and England.

With the drawing of this Love and the voice of this Calling

We shall not cease from exploration
And the end of all our exploring
Will be to arrive where we started
And know the place for the first time.
Through the unknown, remembered gate
When the last of earth left to discover
Is that which was the beginning;
At the source of the longest river
The voice of the hidden waterfall
And the children in the apple-tree
Not known, because not looked for
But heard, half-heard, in the stillness
Between two waves of the sea.
Quick now, here, now, always—
A condition of complete simplicity
(Costing not less than everything)
And all shall be well and

All manner of thing shall be well
When the tongues of flame are in-folded
Into the crowned knot of fire
And the fire and the rose are one.

TRADITION AND THE INDIVIDUAL TALENT

*I*n *English writing we seldom* speak of tradition, though we occasionally apply its name in deploring its absence. We cannot refer to "the tradition" or to "a tradition"; at most, we employ the adjective in saying that the poetry of So-and-so is "traditional" or even "too traditional." Seldom, perhaps, does the word appear except in a phrase of censure. If otherwise, it is vaguely approbative, with the implication, as to the work approved, of some pleasing archaeological reconstruction. You can hardly make the word agreeable to English ears without this comfortable reference to the reassuring science of archaeology.

Certainly the word is not likely to appear in our appreciations of living or dead writers. Every nation, every race, has not only its own creative, but its own critical turn of mind; and is even more oblivious of the shortcomings and limitations of its critical habits than of those of its creative genius. We know, or think we know, from the enormous mass of critical writing that has appeared in the French language the critical method or habit of the French; we only conclude (we are such unconscious people) that the French are "more critical" than we, and sometimes even plume ourselves a little with the fact, as if the French were the less spontaneous. Perhaps they are; but we might remind ourselves that criticism is as inevitable as breathing, and that we should be none the worse for articulating what passes in our minds when we read a book and feel an emotion about it, for criticizing our own minds in their work of criticism. One of the facts that might come to light in this process is our tendency to insist, when we praise a poet, upon those aspects of his work in which he least resembles any one else. In these aspects or parts of his work we pretend to find what is individual, what is the peculiar essence of the man. We dwell with satisfaction upon the poet's difference from his predecessors, especially his immediate predecessors; we endeavour to find something that can be isolated in order to be enjoyed. Whereas if we approach a poet without this prejudice we shall often find that not only the best, but the most individual parts of his work may be those in which the dead poets, his ancestors, assert their immortality most vigorously. And I do not mean the impressionable period of adolescence, but the period of full maturity.

Yet if the only form of tradition, of handing down, consisted in following the ways of the immediate generation before us in a blind or timid adherence to its successes, "tradition" should positively be discouraged. We have seen many such simple currents soon lost in the sand; and novelty is better than repetition. Tradition is a matter of much wider significance. It cannot be inherited, and if you want it you must obtain it by great labour. It involves, in the first place, the historical sense, which we may call nearly indispensable to any one who would continue to be a poet beyond his twenty-fifth year; and the historical sense involves a perception, not only of the pastness of the past, but of its presence; the historical sense compels a man to write not merely with his own generation in his bones, but with a feeling that the whole of the literature of Europe from Homer and within it the whole of the literature of his own country has a simultaneous existence and composes a simultaneous order. This historical sense, which is a sense of the timeless as well as of the temporal and of the timeless and of the temporal together, is what makes a writer traditional. And it is at the same time what makes a writer most acutely conscious of his place in time, of his own contemporaneity.

No poet, no artist of any art, has his complete meaning alone. His significance, his appreciation is the appreciation of his relation to the dead poets and artists. You cannot value him alone; you must set him, for contrast and comparison, among the dead. I mean this as a principle of aesthetic, not merely historical, criticism. The necessity that he shall conform, that he shall cohere, is not onesided; what happens when a new work of art is created is something that happens simultaneously to all the works of art which preceded it. The existing monuments form an ideal order among themselves, which is modified by the introduction of the new (the really new) work of art among them. The existing order is complete before the new work arrives; for order to persist after the supervention of novelty, the *whole* existing order must be, if ever so slightly, altered; and so the relations, proportions, values of each work of art toward the whole are readjusted; and this is conformity between the old and the new. Whoever has approved this idea of order, of the form of European, of English literature will not find it preposterous that the past should be altered by the present as much as the present is directed by the past. And the poet who is aware of this will be aware of great difficulties and responsibilities.

In a peculiar sense he will be aware also that he must inevitably be judged by the standards of the past. I say judged, not amputated, by them; not judged to be as good as, or worse or better than, the dead; and certainly not judged by the canons of dead critics. It is a judgment, a comparison, in which two things are measured by each other. To conform merely would be for the new work not really to conform at all; it would not be new, and would therefore not be a work of art. And we do not quite say that the new is more valuable because it fits in; but its fitting in is a test of its value—a test, it is true, which can only be slowly and cautiously applied, for we are none of us infallible judges of conformity. We say: it appears to conform, and is perhaps individual, or it appears individual, and may conform; but we are hardly likely to find that it is one and not the other.

To proceed to a more intelligible exposition of the relation of the poet to the past: he can neither take the past as a lump, an indiscriminate bolus, nor can he form himself wholly on one or two private admirations, nor can he form himself wholly upon one preferred period. The first course is inadmissible, the second is an important experience of youth, and the third is a pleasant and highly desirable supplement. The poet must be very conscious of the main current, which does not at all flow invariably through the most distinguished reputations. He must be quite aware of the obvious fact that art never improves, but that the material of art is never quite the same. He must be aware that the mind of Europe—the mind of his own country—a mind which he learns in time to be much more important than his own private mind—is a mind which changes, and that this change is a development which abandons nothing *en route*, which does not superannuate either Shakespeare, or Homer, or the rock drawing of the Magdalenian draughtsmen.

That this development, refinement perhaps, complication certainly, is not, from the point of view of the artist, any improvement. Perhaps not even an improvement from the point of view of the psychologist or not to the extent which we imagine; perhaps only in the end based upon a complication in economics and machinery. But the difference between the present and the past is that the conscious present is an awareness of the past in a way and to an extent which the past's awareness of itself cannot show.

Some one said: "The dead writers are remote from us because we *know* so much more than they did." Precisely, and they are that which we know.

I am alive to a usual objection to what is clearly part of my programme for the *métier* of poetry. The objection is that the doctrine requires a ridiculous amount of erudition (pedantry), a claim which can be rejected by appeal to the lives of poets in any pantheon. It will even be affirmed that much learning deadens or perverts poetic sensibility. While, however, we persist in believing that a poet ought to know as much as will not encroach upon his necessary receptivity and necessary laziness, it is not desirable to confine knowledge to whatever can be put into a useful shape for examinations, drawing-rooms, or the still more pretentious modes of publicity. Some can absorb knowledge, the more tardy must sweat for it. Shakespeare acquired more essential history from Plutarch than most men could from the whole British Museum. What is to be insisted upon is that the poet must develop or procure the consciousness of the past and that he should continue to develop this consciousness throughout his career.

What happens is a continual surrender of himself as he is at the moment to something which is more valuable. The progress of an artist is a continual self-sacrifice, a continual extinction of personality.

There remains to define this process of depersonalization and its relation to the sense of tradition. It is in this depersonalization that art may be said to approach the condition of science. I, therefore, invite you to consider, as a suggestive analogy, the action which takes place when a bit of finely filiated platinum is introduced into a chamber containing oxygen and sulphur dioxide.

II

Honest criticism and sensitive appreciation are directed not upon the poet but upon the poetry. If we attend to the confused cries of the newspaper critics and the *susurrus* of popular repetition that follows, we shall hear the names of poets in great numbers; if we seek not Bluebook knowledge but the enjoyment of poetry, and ask for a poem, we shall seldom find it. I have tried to point out the importance of the relation of the poem to other poems by other authors, and suggested the conception of poetry as a living whole of all the poetry that has ever been written. The other aspect of this Impersonal theory of poetry is the relation of the poem to its author. And I hinted, by an analogy, that the mind of the mature poet differs from that of the immature one not precisely in any valuation of "personality," not being necessarily more interesting, or having "more to say," but rather by being a more finely perfected medium in which special, or very varied, feelings are at liberty to enter into new combinations.

The analogy was that of the catalyst. When the two gases previously mentioned are mixed in the presence of a filament of platinum, they form sulphurous acid. This combination takes place only if the platinum is present; nevertheless the newly formed acid contains no trace of platinum, and the platinum itself is apparently unaffected; has remained inert, neutral, and unchanged. The mind of the poet is the shred of platinum. It may partly or exclusively operate upon the experience of the man himself; but, the more perfect the artist, the more completely separate in him will be the man who suffers and the mind which creates; the more perfectly will the mind digest and transmute the passions which are its material.

The experience, you will notice, the elements which enter the presence of the transforming catalyst, are of two kinds: emotions and feelings. The effect of a work of art upon the person who enjoys it is an experience different in kind from any experience not of art. It may be formed out of one emotion, or may be a combination of several; and various feelings, inhering for the writer in particular words or phrases or images, may be added to compose the final result. Or great poetry may be made without the direct use of any emotion whatever: composed out of feelings solely. Canto XV of the *Inferno* (Brunetto Latini) is a working up of the emotion evident in the situation; but the effect, though single as that of any work of art, is obtained by considerable complexity of detail. The last quatrain gives an image, a feeling attaching to an image, which "came," which did not develop simply out of what precedes, but which was probably in suspension in the poet's mind until the proper combination arrived for it to add itself to. The poet's mind is in fact a receptacle for seizing and storing up numberless feelings, phrases, images, which remain there until all the particles which can unite to form a new compound are present together.

If you compare several representative passages of the greatest poetry you see how great is the variety of types of combination, and also how completely any semi-ethical criterion of "sublimity" misses the mark. For it is not the "greatness," the intensity, of the emotions, the components, but the intensity of the artistic process, the pressure, so to speak, under which the fusion takes place, that counts. The episode of Paolo and Francesca employs a definite emotion, but the intensity of the poetry is something quite different from whatever intensity in the supposed experience it may give the impression of. It is no more intense, furthermore, than Canto XXVI, the voyage of Ulysses, which has not the direct dependence upon an emotion. Great variety is possible in the process of transmutation of emotion: the murder of Agamemnon, or the agony of Othello, gives an artistic effect apparently closer to a possible original than the scenes from Dante. In the *Agamemnon,* the artistic emotion approximates to the emotion of an actual spectator; in *Othello* to the emotion of the protagonist himself. But the difference between art and the event is always absolute; the combination which is the murder of Agamemnon is probably as complex as that which is the voyage of Ulysses. In either case there has been a fusion of elements. The ode of Keats contains a number of feelings which have nothing particular to do with the nightingale, but which the nightingale, partly, perhaps, because of its attractive name, and partly because of its reputation, served to bring together.

The point of view which I am struggling to attack is perhaps related to the metaphysical theory of the substantial unity of the soul: for my meaning is, that the poet has, not a "personality" to express, but a particular medium, which is only a medium and not a personality, in which impressions and experiences combine in peculiar and unexpected ways. Impressions and experiences which are important for the man may take no place in the poetry, and those which become important in the poetry may play quite a negligible part in the man, the personality.

I will quote a passage which is unfamiliar enough to be regarded with fresh attention in the light—or darkness—of these observations:

> *And now methinks I could e'en chide myself*
> *For doating on her beauty, though her death*
> *Shall be revenged after no common action.*
> *Does the silkworm expend her yellow labours*
> *For thee? For thee does she undo herself?*
> *Are lordships sold to maintain ladyships*
> *For the poor benefit of a bewildering minute?*
> *Why does yon fellow falsify highways,*
> *And put his life between the judge's lips,*
> *To refine such a thing—keeps horse and men*
> *To beat their valours for her?* . . .

In this passage (as is evident if it is taken in its context) there is a combination of positive and negative emotions: an intensely strong attraction toward beauty and an equally intense fascination by the ugliness which is contrasted with it and which destroys it. This balance of contrasted emotion is in the dramatic situation to which the speech is pertinent, but that situation alone is inadequate to it. This is, so to speak, the structural emotion, provided by the drama. But the whole effect, the dominant tone, is due to the fact that a number of floating feelings, having an affinity to this emotion by no means superficially evident, have combined with it to give us a new art emotion.

It is not in his personal emotions, the emotions provoked by particular events in his life, that the poet is in any way remarkable or interesting. His particular emotions may be simple, or crude, or flat. The emotion in his poetry will be a very complex thing, but not with the complexity of the emotions of people who have very complex or unusual emotions in life. One error, in fact, of eccentricity in poetry is to seek for new human emotions to express; and in this search for novelty in the wrong place it discovers the perverse. The business of the poet is not to find new emotions, but to use the ordinary ones and, in working them up into poetry, to express feelings which are not in actual emotions at all. And emotions which he has never experienced will serve his turn as well as those familiar to him. Consequently, we must believe that "emotion recollected in tranquillity" is an inexact formula. For it is neither emotion, nor recollection, nor, without distortion of meaning, tranquillity. It is a concentration, and a new thing resulting from the concentration, of a very great number of experiences which to the practical and active person would not seem to be experiences at all; it is a concentration which does not happen consciously or of deliberation. These experiences are not "recollected," and they finally unite in an atmosphere which is "tranquil" only in that it is a passive attending upon the event. Of course this is not quite the whole story. There is a great deal, in the writing of poetry, which must be conscious and deliberate. In fact, the bad poet is usually unconscious where he ought to be conscious, and conscious where he ought to be unconscious. Both errors tend to make him "personal." Poetry is not a turning loose of emotion, but an escape from emotion; it is not the expression of personality, but an escape from personality. But, of course, only those who have personality and emotions know what it means to want to escape from these things.

III

δ δε νους ισως Θειοτερον τι και απαθες εστιν

This essay proposes to halt at the frontier of metaphysics or mysticism, and confine itself to such practical conclusions as can be applied by the responsible person interested in poetry. To divert interest from the poet to the poetry is a laudable aim: for it would conduce to a juster estimation of actual poetry, good and bad. There are many people who appreciate the expression of sincere emotion in verse, and there is a smaller number of people who can appreciate technical excellence. But very few know when there is an expression of *significant* emotion, emotion which has its life in the poem and not in the history of the poet. The emotion of art is impersonal. And the poet cannot reach this impersonality without surrendering himself wholly to the work to be done. And he is not likely to know what is to be done unless he lives in what is not merely the present, but the present moment of the past, unless he is conscious, not of what is dead, but of what is already living.

ABOUT THE AUTHORS

T.S. ELIOT (1888–1965) was born in St. Louis, Missouri, attended Harvard University, and later taught in a boys' school briefly before spending eight years at Lloyd Bank in London. In 1935, he entered book publishing, and at the time of his death, he was a director of the English firm Faber and Faber. In 1948, he was awarded the Nobel Prize in Literature.

VIJAY SESHADRI was born in India in 1954 and moved to America as a small child. He is the author of four books of poetry, as well as many essays, reviews, and memoir fragments. His work has been widely published and anthologized and recognized with a number of honors, including the Pulitzer Prize.